THE UNITED NATIONS
AND THE MAINTENANCE OF
INTERNATIONAL SECURITY

The United Nations and the Maintenance of International Security

A Challenge To Be Met

JAMES S. SUTTERLIN

FOREWORD BY BRUCE RUSSETT

PRAEGER

Westport, Connecticut
London

Library of Congress Cataloging-in-Publication Data

Sutterlin, James S.
    The United Nations and the maintenance of international security :
a challenge to be met / James S. Sutterlin ; foreword by Bruce Russett.
        p.   cm.
    Includes bibliographical references and index.
    ISBN 0–275–95052–2 (hard : alk. paper).—ISBN 0–275–95053–0
(pbk. : alk. paper)
    1. Security, International. 2. United Nations. 3. United
Nations—Armed Forces. I. Title.
JX1952.S929 1995
341.5′ 8—dc20   94–40038

British Library Cataloguing in Publication Data is available.

Library of Congress Catalog Card Number: 94–40038
ISBN: 0–275–95052–2
        0–275–95053–0 (pbk.)

First published in 1995

Praeger Publishers, 88 Post Road West, Westport, CT 06881
An imprint of Greenwood Publishing Group, Inc.

Printed in the United States of America

The paper used in this book complies with the
Permanent Paper Standard issued by the National
Information Standards Organization (Z39.48–1984).

10 9 8 7 6 5 4 3 2 1

This book was prepared with the support of a grant from the United States Institute of
Peace.

Chapters 3 and 4 on the use of military force by the United Nations for purposes of peace
are substantially revised versions of papers prepared for the Canadian Centre for Global
Security that were published as No. 18 in its series of Aurora Papers. These chapters also
contain material that was included in "The UN in a New World Order" by Bruce Russett
and James S. Sutterlin in the Spring 1991 edition of *Foreign Affairs*.

An earlier version of Chapter 8 on the Secretary-General as Chief Administrative Officer
was prepared for the Ralph Bunche Institute and was included in *The Challenging Role of the
UN Secretary-General*, edited by Benjamin Rivlin (1993). Westport, CT: Praeger, an imprint of
Greenwood Publishing Group, Inc. Reprinted with permission.

Dedicated to the Core Group:
good colleagues who contributed much to the thinking
in this book

Millions of tongues record thee, and anew
Their children's lips shall echo them, and
say —
"Here, where the sword united nations drew
Our countrymen were warring on that day!"
And this is much, and all which will not
pass away.
—Lord Byron, from *Childe Harold*

Contents

Foreword

Jim Sutterlin introduced himself to me in 1985. At that time he was Executive Director of the Executive Office of the Secretary General of the United Nations—effectively the right-hand person to Mr. Javier Pérez de Cuéllar. Earlier he had served for eight years as Director of the Political Affairs Division of the United Nations under Pérez de Cuéllar and the previous Secretary General, Kurt Waldheim. In those capacities he had witnessed both successes and failures in UN efforts to keep or restore the peace, and had developed many ideas about how the office of the Secretary General, along with various other parts of the United Nations system, might be strengthened. He had the experience and the political sense to know it would not be easy. But he also—as few others at that time—had the intellectual vision to see some possibilities, and to reach out to the academic community for advice in shaping that vision.

This was, however, at the height of the Cold War—a time when the UN was not necessarily highly valued by many policymakers, and when most academic scholarship had turned away from global institutions. I myself had not done serious scholarship on the Untied Nations for almost two decades. In coming to academics in general, and to us at Yale in particular, Jim Sutterlin therefore had to prime a pump that was pretty dry. He did so by graciously seeking our advice even though he may not have expected much of immediate value in return, pulling several of us at Yale into his international network and kindling or rekindling our interest in the possibilities of a stronger United Nations. In doing so he and some young colleagues from the Secretariat organized a series of international conferences on Multilateral Means of Reducing the Risk of War. Those conferences brought together scholars and policymakers who, perhaps to their surprise, found they had much to share, in terms of experience, ideas, and a growing sense that some enhancement of the UN's role in international peace and security might indeed be feasible.

Shortly thereafter he retired from the United Nations service, and was free, as a private citizen, to pursue his ideas and conviction. In 1988 he became a Fellow of the program in International Security Studies at Yale, and began to pursue one of the most vigorous and productive "retirements" I have ever seen. Yale was extremely lucky to have this energetic policy intellectual in its midst. Yale and Sutterlin were both lucky, too, in timing. By then the Cold War was breaking down. The Soviet Union and the United States began to cooperate more, and started to see ways in which the UN might help to stabilize some of the political transformations that were starting to occur. Use of the veto in the Security Council became rare, as the Permanent Members endorsed a wide range of new peacekeeping activities. "New thinkers" under Mikhail Gorbachev were especially open to ideas for enhancing the United Nations. Our international conferences became more wide-ranging, more innovative, and more productive. Many of us were drawn in by the new sense of intellectual excitement and the opportunity for strengthening international institutions.

Operating in part from New Haven, Jim Sutterlin's activities rapidly expanded. He continued to organize conferences—spotting good topics, identifying participants, raising the funding. He conducted an Oral History of the United Nations, based on interviews with some of the founders of the UN and many UN officers and national policymakers; these materials are now on deposit with the Yale University Library. He assisted Mr. Pérez de Cuéllar in the preparation of his memoirs. He continued to be an intellectual catalyst for new ideas and perspectives, and as a special adviser contributed heavily to the first draft of Secretary General Boutros Boutros-Ghali's *An Agenda for Peace*. His contribution to the new public discourse on international security was recognized when he was named Chairman of the Academic Council on the United Nations System, an organization of scholars and policy intellectuals.

As he began to teach at Yale, his seminar restored the study of the United Nations to our undergraduate curriculum. Since then he and I have twice co-taught the first graduate seminar on the United Nations offered here in more than a decade. Currently he is also wise counselor to Paul Kennedy and me as we serve as Co-Directors of the Secretariat for the *Independent Working Group on the United Nations in Its Second Half Century*, and collaborator in a separate project on options for restructuring the Security Council.

There would have been no program in United Nations Studies at Yale without him, and the existing program is rich for his continued deep involvement.

The focus of our earliest discussions was on the possible role of the United Nations in multilateral means of crisis management. This was appropriate to the middle 1980s, when so much attention was devoted to the risks of a Soviet-American nuclear confrontation. His special contributions, however, were to explore ways in which the Secretary General's office might be strengthened both in its capacities for timely information-gathering and in the ability to communicate rapidly in possible mediation with crisis participants. Distinctive also was his concern about multilateral crises, not just since confrontations between small powers might bring the two nuclear superpowers into conflict, but since such confrontations might also bring in other nuclear powers in a much more complex and dangerous interplay than a straight bipolar conflict would imply.

As these fears eased somewhat with the end of the Cold War, he was quick to see that the possible—and necessary—role of the United Nations was much broader. The UN in its most visible manifestations had been focused on collective security enforcement (uniquely, before 1990, in the Korean War) and in traditional peacekeeping; that is, as an impartial force operating with the permission of warring parties who were ready to cease fighting, most often in international conflicts. Jim Sutterlin recognized that future conflicts were likely very often to be located within existing states rather than between them, and to require a much wider range of international capabilities. The focus of a post–Cold War United Nations, he realized, should be on *human security*—not just the security of the states which are members of the United Nations, but the security of populations within states. Transitions to independence or democratic government, humanitarian relief from natural disaster, the prevention and mitigation of civil wars or political chaos, would invite much different kinds of UN activity.

For these, in addition to traditional peacekeeping or peace enforcement, would be needed greater capacities for preventive diplomacy, peacemaking, and peace-building. Peace would require the integration of UN institutions directed toward traditional forms of security from military violence with those parts of the UN concerned with security from poverty and disease and those concerned with the security of political and cultural rights from abuse. These other parts of the UN could be used more effectively to prevent some forms of violent conflict from emerging, could inhibit or halt the escalation of violence, and could be brought together to rebuild shattered societies and economies after the violence was over. Seeing these needs and possibilities, he continually expanded our conceptions of the UN's role in international peace and security before those conceptions became common in public discourse.

The comprehensiveness of this book illustrates the comprehensiveness of Jim Sutterlin's view. As a senior officer in the United States Foreign Service he developed an appreciation of his country's interest, and as an international civil servant he demonstrated how that interest could be maintained yet transcended. His commitment to a wide and longterm perspective on the national interest and his normative commitment to an inclusive human interest will both be evident to the reader. I am grateful for the gift of providence that brought him to this understanding, that brought him to our intellectual community at Yale, and that continues to bring his wisdom to the global community.

Bruce Russett

1

Old Principles, New Realities

For millennia humans have sought formulas for the maintenance of their security and the peaceful settlement of their conflicts. Each historic era has witnessed the emergence of new ideas—or the reemergence of old—in the hope that the mistakes of the past would not be repeated. With the end of the Cold War the world has entered again such a period of questioning and exploration.

A NEW PARADIGM

The paradigm of international relations has changed so significantly that it is fair to say that a new era has begun, one that offers hope, but no certainty, that the failed dreams of the past can be realized. A rare and still fragile unanimity has become evident: that this new era demands a multilateral approach to the resolution of its problems, some inherited from the past, some born in the chaos of adjustment to new conditions of wider freedom, of hatreds reborn, and of growing challenges to the habitat required for human security.

The United Nations has come to the fore as the instrument of choice to bring peace and productive change. With its new prominence has come proof of enhanced effectiveness and unprecedented responsibilities, along with evidence of imperfections and unpreparedness. The United Nations, after all, was born for a different era, the inheritor of many of the norms and a portion of the structure of an organization, the League of Nations, that had failed. To what extent is this fifty-year-old organization competent to provide security for a new generation of humanity? Where did the concepts that have determined its history originate? How need the United Nations be changed and strengthened? Are the purposes and principles on which it was founded relevant and adequate for the realities of this new era? These are the questions with which the present book is concerned.

PRINCIPLES OF THE PAST

Not until the League of Nations was established at the end of World War I was a structure formed in which the majority of the nations of the world were joined in a commonly accepted responsibility for the maintenance of world peace—not peace within a certain region, as had been the case in the Concert of Europe, but peace among all countries. The members of the League were joined, too, in norms of international behavior defined in the League Covenant and in the commitment to take common action, including the automatic application of sanctions against any "Covenant-breaking" country. Thus, for the first time, norms and structure with universal application were combined in a multilateral organization that had for its principal purpose the maintenance of peace.

Central to the potential effectiveness of this organization was the concept of collective security, which is, in essence, the simple principle that all countries will undertake common action against any country that threatens the security of another state—simple, in concept, but extraordinarily difficult in practice. The United Nations took over these ideas as its own; it assumed the same global responsibility for the maintenance of international peace and security even though the founders were fully aware that the League had failed. The American Under Secretary of State, Sumner Welles, had already declared in 1941 that the League "had never been able, as intended, to bring about peaceful and equitable adjustments between nations. . . . Some adequate instrumentality must unquestionably be found to achieve such adjustments when the nations of the earth again undertake the task of restoring law and order to a disastrously shaken world."[1]

A year later, Secretary of State Cordell Hull declared in a radio address that "it is plain to see that some international agency must be created which can—by force, if necessary—keep the peace among nations in the future. There must be international cooperative action to set up the mechanisms that can thus insure peace."[2] The problem was to avoid those mistakes and inadequacies that had prevented the League from achieving this goal. There were a good many reasons for the League's failure (it had successes as well), but the most important in terms of multilateral effectiveness today were 1) the failure of important states to comply with the provisions of the Covenant, 2) the absence from the League of major states (the United States never joined, the Soviet Union joined late and was subsequently expelled when it invaded Finland, and Germany, Japan and Italy all withdrew), 3) the ineffectiveness of the means of enforcement action against covenant-breaking states, and, closely related, 4) the readiness of governments—in particular the permanent members of the Council—in resisting aggression, to place perceived national interests above the common interest of the world community as represented by the League.

STRENGTHENING THE PRINCIPLES OF THE LEAGUE

To overcome these weaknesses the capacity of the new organization to enforce action against aggression and threats to peace needed to be stronger. With this objective, the unconditional provision was included that all members would accept and carry out the decisions of the Security Council (Article 25 of the Charter). Further, "in order to contribute to the maintenance of international peace and security," members would undertake to make available to the Security Council armed forces, assistance and facilities, in accordance with special agreements to be completed with each member, to be used by the Council to maintain or restore international security. Members were to hold national air force contingents immediately available for combined international enforcement action. A Military Staff Committee was established to advise and assist the Security Council on all questions relating to military requirements for the maintenance of international peace and security and the employment and command of forces placed at its disposal.[3] Thus member states were clearly committed to accept and carry out the decisions of the Security Council, which would act in behalf of the members in the maintenance of international peace and security. The members would provide the necessary troops and logistic support for the Council to do this.[4]

The second cause of the failure of the League of Nations that had to be overcome was the nonparticipation of major countries, especially the United States. To gain the approval of the U.S. Senate, the prerequisite for American membership, it had to be clearly established that action could not be taken to maintain international security that might engage the United States in enforcement action without the concurrence of the United States Government. For this reason, the U.S. plan for the United Nations provided that the Security Council would have primary responsibility for the maintenance of international security and that only the decisions of the Council would be binding on member states. Any such decisions, except on procedural matters, would require the affirmative vote of the five permanent members of the Council, the permanent members being China, France, the United Kingdom, the Soviet Union and the United States. In other words, a permanent member could veto any action proposed in the Council that it perceived as contrary to its interests, unless it was a party to the dispute and enforcement action was not involved.[5]

Two central features of the League of Nations were taken over intact. The United Nations was to be an organization of sovereign states without any aspects of supranationality and it would have no authority to intervene in the domestic affairs of member states.

One concept of enormous importance was added that distinguished the UN from the League: the concept that satisfaction of the economic, cultural and humanitarian needs of the global population was an essential element in the maintenance of peace between states. The UN Charter speaks in this context of the objectives of social progress, especially respect for human rights and better standards of life in larger freedom. The U.S. Secretary of State, Edward Stettinius, in his final report on the Charter to President Truman put it succinctly: "The battle of peace has to be fought on two fronts. The first is the security front where victory spells freedom from fear. The second is the economic and social front where victory means freedom from want."[6]

During its first fifty years the dominant portion of the UN's resources was to be devoted to this "second front." However, to a large extent, economic and social development came to be seen as objectives in themselves separate from the UN's primary objective of the maintenance of international security. Now, as the definition of international security has broadened to encompass not only peace between states but also the security of populations within states, economic and social progress are increasingly seen again as essential to international security. The realization, or nonrealization, of these original principles on which the United Nations was based, their observance, or nonobservance, and now, increasingly, their interpretation, will define the capacity of the United Nations to deal with the threat and the reality of conflict in the changed circumstances of the post–Cold War world.

CAN PAST WEAKNESSES BE OVERCOME?

Looking to the past, the United Nations, despite these well-considered principles and concepts, was not, for most of its history, very effective in realizing the objectives of the Charter. The protection afforded the Permanent Members by the right of veto during this period surely was instrumental in their remaining in the United Nations even when their positions were under severe attack. Now that the permanent members of the Security Council are cooperating effectively in the interest of preserving peace, we

can see how important it was that they should remain in the organization
during the long period of discord and drought. This marks a very positive
contrast with the experience of the League of Nations and can be seen as a
persuasive justification for the much maligned veto. But this was hardly
apparent in the long years during which the Security Council was para-
lyzed by the Cold War.

The sad lesson of those years is that a system of collective security that
is heavily dependent on decisions to be taken by the Security Council and,
in extremis, militarily enforced by the Council, cannot work effectively
unless the permanent members are in agreement. For most of the first forty
years of the history of the United Nations they were not. The agreements
with member states on the provision of troops and facilities for use by the
Security Council provided for in Article 43 of the UN Charter were never
reached in large part because of disagreement between the United States
and the Soviet Union on the structure and mission such a force would have.
Even those decisions that were reached by the Council were frequently
ignored even by Council members. Conflicts were numerous and widespread. As a partial answer, the United Nations developed the technique of
peacekeeping; but this was intended to control a conflict situation after,
rather than before, conflict had occurred.

It appeared that, apart from keeping all the principal members in the
organization, the changes introduced in the United Nations had not made
it much more effective in maintaining peace than the League had been. By
1982 Secretary-General Javier Pérez de Cuéllar warned in his first annual
report to the General Assembly that

> The Council seems powerless. . . . The process of peaceful settlement
> of disputes prescribed in the Charter is often brushed aside. . . .
> Sterner measures for world peace were envisaged in Chapter VII of
> the Charter, which was conceived as a key element of the United
> Nations system of collective security, but the prospect of realizing
> such measures is now deemed almost impossible in our divided
> international community. We are perilously near to a new interna-
> tional anarchy.[7]

The Secretary-General was right in his immediate assessment. What he
overlooked was that the provisions of the Charter for the maintenance of
international security that had proved so ineffective during the arid years
of the Cold War, could and would become effective, at least for a while, once
the Cold War ended. The application of military force to preserve peace and
prevent massive violations of human rights became possible, the injunction
against intervention in the domestic affairs of states became subject to
reinterpretation and the United Nations became engaged in the complex
undertaking of peace-building. This new potential of the United Nations,

as seen in the use of military force, the process of peace-building, the control of nuclear weapons, the role of the Secretary-General and of regional organizations and the ways in which this new potential can be realized are themes in each of the chapters of this book.

A TIME OF PROGRESS

The years since 1987 have seen significant accomplishments in all of these areas. After the advent to power in the Soviet Union of Mikhail Gorbachev the prospects for an effective Security Council changed significantly. With his policy of conciliation with the West, of "de-ideologizing relations among states"[8] and of strong support for the United Nations, he opened the possibility for cooperation among the Permanent Members of the Council in dealing with regional conflicts and disputes. Recognizing the importance of this possibility, Secretary-General Javier Pérez de Cuéllar brought the representatives of the five permanent members together in March 1987 and called for their joint efforts to end the war between Iraq and Iran, which at that point threatened to spread and directly involve the United States and the Soviet Union. The Five cooperated, and with the quiet encouragement and assistance of the Secretary-General, together developed the elements for a cease-fire between the two countries that were incorporated in a Security Council resolution on the basis of which the war was finally ended. This collaboration among the permanent members, while not widely noted at the time, marked the beginning of a new era for the United Nations.

The agreement on the terms for the cease-fire between Iran and Iraq was followed in quick succession by agreement in the Security Council on the UN plan for Namibia's transition to independence, on the UN's political and military role in the Central American peace process, on the ambitious plan for bringing peace and stability to Cambodia and in 1990, by the historic decision to repel by force Iraq's invasion of Kuwait. In the case of Central America, the United States made a notable change in its longstanding policy by agreeing to a peace plan in the implementation of which the United Nations would have the central role. The United States had never been willing to rely on the United Nations—nor, indeed, to see the United Nations very deeply involved—in Central America or the Caribbean as long as it saw this area as one where the Soviet Union was seeking to expand its influence, convinced that communism posed a threat to the hemisphere. This change could hardly have happened without the "de-ideologization of international relations" of which Gorbachev spoke.

The positive influence of the end of the Cold War on the effectiveness of the Security Council went beyond the achievement of agreement on Council resolutions. Since the United States and the Soviet Union were no longer in the position of rival sponsors of countries or internal elements involved in conflict, their influence could be applied on a national basis in tandem with the multilateral decisions of the Council in order to encourage implementation of Council decisions. The commonality of interests in the prevention and resolution of regional conflicts that developed between the great powers placed them finally on the side of the basic objective of the United Nations. In these new international circumstances the United Sates could recognize that a UN-brokered peace in Central America served the national interests of the United States, just as the Soviet Union could see that the UN umbrella provided for the withdrawal of Soviet forces from Afghanistan served its national interests as well as those of the international community.

NEW CHALLENGES

The new coincidence of the interests of the five permanent members of the Security Council and the accordance of these interests with the objectives of the UN Charter were hopeful harbingers of what both American President Bush and Soviet President Gorbachev referred to as a new world order. But it was soon apparent that the new world order had some highly problematic aspects. Most significantly, the nature of the threats to peace and of conflict assumed characteristics for which the founders of the UN had not planned and with which the UN was not well prepared to deal. The Charter of the United Nations was drafted in the expectation that the Security Council would act to prevent, or to stop, interstate war—wars fought between national armies across national boundaries. When the Security Council finally gained the extent of agreement among its permanent members needed to act effectively against such events, most conflicts in the world stemmed from societal roots rather than rivalry between states, and they were essentially internal—*intrastate*—in nature. Iraq's invasion of Kuwait was, of course, the old-fashioned kind of war, a vivid indication that this type of threat to the peace cannot be ruled out in the future. But aside from the Gulf War, the conflict situations with which the Council has sought to deal in the post–Cold War era have been essentially intrastate in nature, albeit with implications going far beyond national borders.

The Central American peace process required not peace between states, but peace between warring factions within Nicaragua and El Salvador. In Cambodia, the United Nations plan to restore stability and freedom entailed supervision of civil administration, the resettlement of refugees and the disarmament of the various armed forces operating in the country. The complexity of the problem of maintaining international security in the post–Cold War world was tragically illustrated by the conflict that broke out in what had been Yugoslavia. There, latent nationalism within the federated republics of Slovenia and Croatia, combined with hostility and distrust between the ethnic societies within Yugoslavia, caused Slovenia and Croatia to declare their independence, to be followed shortly thereafter by Bosnia-Herzegovina and Macedonia. The nature of the ensuing armed conflict and the involvement of the UN will be examined in some detail in a later chapter. It suffices here to note that the United Nations found it necessary, in the interest of peace and the provision of humanitarian assistance, to perform peacekeeping functions between factions within a (newly declared) state; peacemaking functions to bring a solution between the new states; protective functions, within conditions of civil war, to bring humanitarian assistance to the needy population; and all of this in cooperation with the regional organizations that were involved in the peace efforts.

The United Nations, even in the new conditions of harmony among the permanent members of the Security Council, was not prepared to meet all the new demands that this situation imposed, a situation partially replicated in several of the former republics of the Soviet Union. Other conflicts followed in Somalia, Haiti and Rwanda that highlighted the manifold questions that arise when the UN undertakes to bring an end to such a massive infringement of basic human rights as to constitute a threat to international security. The Gulf War illustrated the inability of the Security Council to field a UN fighting force under UN command to repel aggression by a major national army. The chaotic conflict in Somalia illustrated the opposite problem of the inadequacy of the command and control capacity of the United Nations to successfully carry out an internal enforcement action even when it was able to deploy a significant military force.

Other difficult questions arose as the Security Council and the Secretary-General struggled to deal with the new problems that arose one after another in these conflicts. What are the criteria for intervention? What policy should the UN follow if one of the parties to a conflict that had given consent to UN intervention takes hostile action against UN forces (as happened in Somalia)? Are sanctions a proper means of enforcement if great hardship results for the innocent civilian population (as in Haiti)?

In the face of these dilemmas, the newly effective Security Council seemed at times to lose its sense of direction. The problem that had proved fatal to the League—the unwillingness of the major powers to subordinate their national interests to the wider interests represented by the League Covenant—again arose when the United States declared that it would not participate in peacekeeping or peace-enforcement actions unless it could be clearly shown that participation was in the American national interest.

DEFINING NEW RULES OF THE GAME

The Security Council recognized that a rethinking of old rules and guidelines and the development of new approaches were needed to take full advantage of the opportunities for peace that a new era in international relations offered. Meeting in January, 1991, for the first time in its history at the level of heads of state and government, the Council issued a statement noting that the ending of the Cold War "has raised hopes for a safer, more equitable and more humane world." After reaffirming the commitment of Council members "to the collective security system of the Charter to deal with threats to peace and to reverse acts of aggression," the Council invited the Secretary-General to provide "his analysis and recommendations on ways of strengthening and making more efficient within the framework and provisions of the Charter the capacity of the United Nations for preventive diplomacy, for peacemaking and for peace-keeping."[9]

Secretary-General Boutros-Ghali responded in a wide-ranging report entitled *An Agenda for Peace*. Many of the recommendations that he put forward will be considered in the relevant chapters of this book. In the Introduction he reminded all member states that "the search for improved mechanisms and techniques will be of little significance unless this new spirit of commonality is propelled by the will to take the hard decisions demanded by this time of opportunity."[10] Many of the decisions that are desirable are, indeed, hard since some, such as redefining the limits of sovereignty, touch on questions that may not lend themselves to clearly defined answers. Other problems, such as better coordination of the programs of the UN system for the purpose of peace-building, have been under examination for years without a satisfactory solution being found. But the present constellation of international relations, despite the manifold apparent problems, is the most fortuitous for enhanced effectiveness that the United Nations has enjoyed. It affords an opportunity to adapt the sound principles on which the United Nations was founded to the vastly altered circumstances of a changed world. This is the recurrent theme of the ensuing chapters in which examination is made of the capacity and potential of the United Nations to maintain international security and to build peace on into the next century.

NOTES

1. Ruth Russell, *History of the United Nations Charter* (Washington, D.C.: The Brookings Institution, 1958), p. 32.
2. Ibid.
3. United Nations Charter, Chapter VII, Articles 42, 43, 45, 47.
4. United Nations Charter, Chapter V, Articles 24, 25.
5. In practice this provision, as incorporated in Article 27 of the UN Charter, has been interpreted to mean that only a negative vote by a permanent member constitutes a veto. A resolution may be adopted if one or more permanent members abstain or are absent.

6. Edward R. Stettinius, Jr., *Report to the President on the Results of the San Francisco Conference* (Department of State, June 26, 1945), p. 109.

7. Javier Pérez de Cuéllar, *Anarchy or Order* (New York: United Nations, 1991), p. 6.

8. See the speech of Mikhail Gorbachev to the UN General Assembly December 7, 1988, printed in the *New York Times*, December 8, 1988, p. A16.

9. General Assembly Document S/23500, 31 January 1992.

10. Boutros-Ghali, *An Agenda for Peace* (New York: United Nations, 1992), p. 3.

2

Preventing Conflict

It is often said that it is easier to prevent war than to deal with its consequences. This, unfortunately, is difficult to prove. Successes are hard to confirm whereas every war and conflict is evidence of failure. Since there have been so many armed conflicts, widely spread through many regions, in the past half century, one can only conclude that the effectiveness of the United Nations in preventing conflict—a major purpose for which it was created—needs at the very least enhancement. The United Nations has, in reality, been singularly unsuccessful in taking the preventive steps that might arrest a conflict before it reaches the level of armed exchange.

Successive Secretaries-General have called for improvement in the preventive diplomacy capacity of the organization. In his 1989 report to the General Assembly on the work of the organization, Javier Pérez de Cuéllar wrote the following:

> The prevention of armed conflicts is a mandate envisaged in the provisions of the Charter relating both to the Security Council and the responsibilities of the Secretary-General. Article 34 speaks of any situation which might lead to international friction or give rise to a dispute and Article 99 of any matter which, in the Secretary-General's opinion, may threaten the maintenance of international peace and security. However, as has been repeatedly observed, it has been the

general practice over the years to address a particular situation only
after it has clearly taken a turn toward the use of force.[1]

One of the three things for which the 1992 Summit Meeting of the Security
Council requested the analysis and suggestions of the Secretary-General
was a means of enhancing the effectiveness of the United Nations in
preventive diplomacy.

Why has the United Nations been largely unsuccessful until now in this
function? How can its performance be improved? To cite a tragic example:
Why didn't, or couldn't, the United Nations prevent the fratricidal war from
breaking out in Bosnia? The answers, to the extent they exist, derive first
from the nature of conflict that is to be anticipated and second from the
diplomatic tools and the degree of authority available to the United Nations
in the given circumstances.

THE NEED FOR "PREVENTIVE MEASURES"

Conflict between any of the permanent members of the Security Council,
or between major industrial powers, which inevitably would take on global
dimensions, was a terrible nightmare but never a likely reality even during
the Cold War. Now it is highly improbable. It can be reasonably assumed
that in the future, even as now, the conflicts that the United Nations should
be in a position to prevent will be regional, and in this geographic sense,
limited in nature. They may stem from interstate disputes (as, for example,
between India and Pakistan over Kashmir, or between two African countries because of colonial-era borders). More, however, are likely to stem
from societal tensions *within* countries or sub-regions, and consequently,
will be of an internal, domestic nature. The United Nations must be in a
position to prevent conflicts of either kind.

Dealing with possible internal conflict is something for which no guidelines exist in the UN Charter. The most relevant provision is Article 2,
Paragraph 7, which states that "Nothing contained in the present Charter
shall authorize the United Nations to intervene in matters which are essentially within the domestic jurisdiction of any state." This is obviously
restrictive rather than enabling. Any measures to prevent *intrastate* conflict
have to be planned and undertaken with this provision much in mind. Yet,
if conflicts continue to be predominantly internal in nature, the United
Nations cannot meet its mandate to preserve peace without dealing with
them—without seeking in every appropriate way to prevent or mitigate
social tensions that derive from such factors as ethnic or religious division
or human rights violations, before they escalate into armed violence. Preventive diplomacy, as a result, needs to take forms, such as the resettlement
of populations or the training of police forces, that normally would be

considered outside the scope of diplomacy. For this reason "preventive measures" is a more accurate term than "preventive diplomacy" for what is needed to prevent conflict today.

INFORMATION AND ANALYSIS

There are certain requirements that apply in general to the prevention of conflict, whether it be interstate or intrastate in nature. The first is timely information and perceptive analysis. It is patently impossible to prevent something if there is no knowledge that it might happen or inadequate understanding of its causes and possible cures. The United Nations does not have, and is not likely to have, an intelligence operation because governments do not relish being spied on by their own organization. The United Nations is therefore dependent on information provided by governments (often to the Secretary-General), by the world media, by academic and institutional sources, by incoming information from UN field posts (a minor source until now except in countries where peacekeeping operations are under way) and by official government declarations, statements and statistics. These sources, if they are well exploited and analyzed, can in many cases provide an early indication of regional tension and its causes. However, the capacity of the United Nations Secretariat to assimilate and analyze information that is available and get it to the Secretary-General or the Security Council for action has been inadequate. Moreover, vital intelligence information of a classified nature has frequently not been available to the United Nations.

Two examples may serve to illustrate the past inadequacy of the early warning system—first, in terms of alert analysis, and second, in terms of the nonavailability of crucial information.

The dispute between Argentina and the United Kingdom over the Falkland Islands had been before the United Nations for many years before Argentina invaded the Islands on March 31, 1982. The positions of the two countries were fully documented in the records of the General Assembly's Decolonization Committee. Moreover, the two governments had held bilateral talks on their dispute in New York, the last session of which adjourned at the end of February, 1982. A communiqué was issued stating that the talks had taken place in a cordial and positive spirit. The resolve of both sides to find a solution to the sovereignty issue was reaffirmed. There appeared no cause, then, for concern. But on March 1, the Argentine Foreign Ministry put out a statement indicating that unless there was an early solution Argentina would choose freely "the procedure that best accorded with its interest."

While this was an official, public statement, it was not reported by the UN Information Center in Buenos Aires and it was not noted in the UN

Secretariat in New York. At almost the same time, a scrap metal merchant arrived on South Georgia Island (which was administered by the United Kingdom as a dependency of the Falklands) aboard an Argentine naval vessel and promptly raised the Argentine flag. London reacted sharply, claiming that the scrap metal workers were illegally occupying British territory and sent its sole naval vessel in the area, with twenty-four marines aboard, to remove the scrap metal workers. Meanwhile Argentina withdrew most of the metal workers but sent another naval vessel with a detachment of marines to protect those who had been left on the Island. At this point there were public reports that Argentina was assembling a task force to invade the Falkland Islands.

The developments on South Georgia were widely reported in the press and were known in the UN Secretariat. However, there was no office in the Secretariat responsible for following and analyzing such developments in the context of the previous history of the problem and the political environment in the two countries involved. No one in the Secretariat raised a warning flag. Not having been alerted, Secretary-General Pérez de Cuéllar, who was in Europe at the time, did not use his good offices with the parties to try to prevent a conflict or bring the matter to the attention of the Security Council as a potential threat to peace and security. The Secretary-General, being from Peru, would have been in a position to communicate effectively with the Argentine leadership. Senior Argentine and British representatives who were in influential positions at the time have indicated that in the face of a warning from the Security Council, both countries would have drawn back from confrontation and Argentina would not have gone ahead with the invasion.[2] This conclusion is bound to be speculative, but it does indicate the need for timely information and, equally important, for acute analysis in the UN Secretariat on developments that could lead to war.

The Iraqi invasion of Kuwait in August, 1990, provides an illustration of the problem that can arise from a lack of access to crucial information. Secretary-General Pérez de Cuéllar was aware in midsummer 1990 of growing tension between Iraq and Kuwait. He knew that Iraq had moved some troops toward the Kuwaiti border. He did not know, however, of the magnitude of the troop movements and therefore had no reason to anticipate an early invasion. Well-informed Arab contacts told him that this was highly unlikely.

Both the United States and the Soviet Union knew from satellite photography the size of the Iraqi buildup, but they did not raise the issue in the Security Council nor did they inform the Secretary-General. Pérez de Cuéllar has stated that if he had had this information he would have gone to the Security Council, as he is authorized to do under Article 99 of the Charter, in order to warn of a threat to peace. He believes, on the basis of the extensive conversations he had subsequently with Saddam Hussein and the Iraqi Deputy Prime Minister, Tariq Assiz, that Saddam Hussein had concluded from his experience when Iraq invaded Iran that, in the case of Kuwait, the Security Council would again take no early action. This was not an illogical conclusion on his part. Even a public warning from the Council, or the dispatch of a small UN fact-finding mission might have, in the view of Pérez de Cuéllar, been sufficient to disillusion Saddam Hussein and persuade him to think twice, at least, before proceeding.[3]

This, too, is entirely speculative but the point is nonetheless persuasive. The Secretary-General needs to have access to intelligence information from member states on developing crises so that he can take whatever preventive action is possible. Secretary-General Boutros-Ghali called for this in *An Agenda for Peace*. The initial response from member states was positive but limitations are likely to remain. Confidentiality has always been a problem in the United Nations given the multinational character of the Secretariat. While this concern on the part of the United States and Russia has decreased with the end of the Cold War, many countries would be extremely resentful if they learned that the Secretary-General was being given intelligence information regarding their internal or external disputes by a third country. Therefore, such information can only be passed with discretion directly to the Secretary-General or to one of his immediate associates, a practice that has now begun but only on an *ad hoc* basis.

Secretary-General Pérez de Cuéllar took several steps to improve the availability of political information and analysis for preventive diplomacy purposes. He first enlarged the mandate of the more than sixty UN Information Centers around the world, to give responsibility to the directors for the submission of regular reports on political developments relevant to the maintenance of international security. This had very limited success. Because of the sensitivity of the host countries, the reports had to be based entirely on unclassified sources. Moreover, many directors were preoccupied with other duties and some had no concept of the nature of political reporting.

Subsequently, Pérez de Cuéllar established as part of his own staff an Office for Research and the Collection of Information (ORCI) with the specific purpose of enhancing the preventive diplomacy capacity of the United Nations. Its mandate was to collect, organize and analyze political information received from all available sources, including the academic community with which it was to maintain continuing contact. On this basis it was to advise the Secretary-General of threatening developments. The Office encountered bureaucratic resistance from other Secretariat departments that were fearful of encroachment on their territory. Moreover, there was insufficient managerial skill to mold the generally gifted staff into a collegial entity that could provide the Secretary-General with the timely counsel that was needed. It served, however, as a valuable and much needed conduit to the international academic community from which considerable value was gained.

Secretary-General Boutros-Ghali, intent on introducing extensive reforms in the Secretariat shortly after assuming his position, decided to
eliminate ORCI. At the same time, he recognized the need for information
and analysis in preventive diplomacy and peacemaking, and so assigned
this function to the newly consolidated Department of Political Affairs. The
General Assembly in its response to *An Agenda for Peace* subsequently
invited the Secretary-General "to strengthen the capacity of the Secretariat
for the collection of information and analysis to serve better the early-warn-
ing needs of the Organization and, to that end, encourages the Secretary-
General to ensure that staff members receive proper training in all aspects
of preventive diplomacy, including the collection and analysis of information."[4] Such a training program for selected staff members has been initiated by the United Nations Institute for Training and Research in Geneva
in cooperation with the International Peace Academy.

THE INFORMATION REQUIREMENTS OF A NEW ERA

Given the prominence of social and economic catalysts in conflict in
today's world, information and analyses encompassing only political factors are bound to be inadequate for preventive purposes. Economic and
social factors need to be incorporated in assessing both the potential for
conflict in a particular region or country and the most effective means of
averting it. The United Nations system does not lack for sources of this type
of information. It is represented in practically every country of the world
and field representatives of functional agencies are well informed on local
economic and social developments that could lead to conflict or humanitarian crises. A system is needed that would permit advantage to be taken
of this source of "early warning" information—something that has been
developed with regard to crop prospects and, to a limited extent, with
regard to potential refugee flows.

Social, economic and political factors need to be "synthesized," as Boutros-Ghali has suggested, in assessing the need for preventive action and
deciding the appropriate measures to be taken. This could be accomplished
through the establishment of a special "watch" or "early warning" staff in
the UN Secretariat to follow information and reports on political, social and
economic developments from the various sources available to the United
Nations, including the specialized agencies and the functional offices of the
United Nations Organization. Such a staff, which would need to be interdisciplinary, would have the responsibility to alert the Secretary-General
and, through him, the Security Council and ECOSOC as appropriate, on
threatening developments that might call for preventive measures by the
United Nations. The staff would also serve as a policy-planning staff,
providing in-depth analyses of the underlying causes of tension and of the

various options for action by one or more UN organs and agencies and by other organizations. In its recommendations the staff would need to take into account the possibility of utilizing peacekeeping for deterrence purposes—as discussed in the next chapter—but contingency planning for peacekeeping operations should remain the responsibility of the Peacekeeping Department of the Secretariat that established an office for this purpose in mid-1993.

THE ECONOMIC AND SOCIAL DIMENSIONS

Information and analyses, no matter how timely and acute, cannot in themselves, prevent conflict. This is dependent on consequent action. Under present procedures, information and advice on political developments is given directly to the Secretary-General by the heads of departments who make up his "cabinet." Primary responsibility in this regard rests with the Department for Political Affairs. (This, of course, is in addition to the extensive information he receives from his wide-ranging contacts with senior government representatives and other well-informed individuals.) The Secretary-General may, within his political mandate under the Charter, act independently, using his good offices in an effort to alleviate the situation. He may also, either informally, or formally under the provisions of Article 99 of the Charter, bring a situation to the attention of the Security Council as a threat to international peace and security.

There are, however, limitations on the capacity of the Secretary-General, acting independently, to prevent conflict. He has only the power of persuasion. He can recommend but he cannot initiate measures for conflict deterrence such as the deployment of peacekeeping forces that might persuade the parties to resolve their differences peacefully, nor can he threaten enforcement measures under Chapter VII of the Charter. Only the Security Council can take such action. The failures of the past forty years have shown that without authoritative support from the Security Council the prevention of conflict is at best doubtful. There would be good reason, then, for the Council to have collectively available to it, on a continuing basis, information on developments that could lead to conflict.

The word "collectively" is important. The permanent members and some other countries may be adequately informed through national sources. But smaller countries on the Council do not have this advantage. They would, as a rule, be more prepared to vote in favor of preventive action on the basis of information from an independent source. The regular provision to the Council of information relevant to the maintenance of international security, with, as appropriate, comments and recommendations of the Secretary-General, would serve to alert the Council and afford it the opportunity—and impose on it a certain additional obligation—to become involved at an early stage in seeking to prevent conflict. Toward this objective a system should be developed under which information deemed significant is forwarded to the Council on a regular schedule as well as on an ad hoc basis by the Secretary-General if a particularly threatening situation needs to be highlighted.

The Economic and Social Council (ECOSOC) is required under the Charter to assist the Security Council on the Council's request.[5] The Security Council can therefore call on ECOSOC for information and reports on economic and social developments relevant to the maintenance of international security. The Council has never until now made such a request but there have been indications that it may do so in the future. Even if this occurs, it will not lessen the need for analyses and advice from the Secretary-General in which all factors—political, military, economic and social—have been taken into account.

The Security Council also has the possibility, as does the Secretary-General, of sending a fact-finding mission to an area of tension to seek information on the basis of which the Council can decide what preventive action can be taken. In recommending that greater use be made of fact-finding, Secretary-General Boutros-Ghali has pointed out that the dispatch of such a mission can, in itself, sometimes serve a preventive purpose by giving a clear indication to the parties of the United Nations's concern and by providing a temporary UN presence in the area that can encourage de-escalation of tension.

MEDIATION

The second requirement for success in preventing conflict—after full and timely information and analysis—is mediation skill. In conflict situations where armed exchange has occurred the United Nations has shown over the years a commendable mediation capability. This has been seen in recent memory in the achievement by the Secretary-General or his representative of an understanding on the withdrawal of Soviet forces from Afghanistan, realization of the cease-fire in the Iran-Iraq war and the negotiation of a settlement of the civil strife in El Salvador. Other instances could be cited of skillful mediation even though the results were not satisfactory. Moreover, reinforcement of the UN's in-house capacity is easily available as in the enlistment of Olaf Palme in the Iran-Iraq war and Cyrus Vance in the Yugoslav crisis. In the past, panels of experts for inquiry and conciliation as well as for fact-finding have been established by the General Assembly.[6] They have almost never been used but they can be revived at any time. The failures in preventing *interstate* conflict have not resulted from inadequate mediation means. There is no lack of skilled mediators available to the United Nations.

It needs to be recognized, however, that a different kind of mediation expertise is needed to deal with strife deriving from social tensions within a society. This is an area where the United Nations has only begun to acquire experience. The United Nations and regional organizations should both have available the expertise and the well-suited personnel that can help to remove or alleviate sources of potential conflict. Mediation in situations of domestic tension can only be afforded at the invitation of the government or of the parties concerned. But the Secretary-General or one of the other organs of the UN can take the initiative in suggesting the utility of third party mediation or conciliation. The Secretary-General could develop a pool of "social conciliators" (as could regional organizations) and indicate the availability of this service and its merits in resolving a particular situation. It must be recognized that UN assistance will not always be accepted by governments and that there will be situations in which the UN cannot be helpful but this should not be interpreted as meaning the approach is not worth pursuing.

LEVERAGE

Leverage can be seen as the third essential element in preventive diplomacy. No matter how skillful the mediator may be, conflict prevention often requires the application of some form of pressure if it is to succeed. Such leverage, whether in the form of proffered benefits or threatened punishment, is largely dependent on action by the Security Council, the General Assembly, UN functional organizations (for the provision of benefits) or from member states. One looks first to the Security Council in this connection since it has primary responsibility for the maintenance of peace.

The Security Council cannot impose a solution to an interstate or intrastate dispute either before or after armed conflict occurs. This possibility was debated at the San Francisco Conference in 1945 and intentionally excluded from the Council's mandate. However, the Council now has means of persuasion—or dissuasion—that during the period of the Cold War were practically nonexistent. The great advantage offered by Council action derives from the possibility of bringing to bear the *combined* influence of its members, thus intensifying the effect and, of at least equal importance, helping to ensure that the permanent members of the Council do not find themselves acting to contrary purpose in a given dispute, as was usually the case during the first four decades of the UN's history.

Governments, before embarking on an adventuresome policy, must now take into account the real possibility that the Council may, if necessary, agree on enforcement measures to maintain international security. The new credibility of Council action translates into substantial leverage that can be applied for preventive purposes. For this leverage to be sustained, the members of the Council, and other member states on the request of the Council, must adjust their national policies toward the parties to a dispute so as to support the objectives agreed on and articulated by the Security Council.

Given the leverage that derives from a Security Council recognized as capable of effective action, there are a range of preventive measures that the Security Council can undertake with reasonable hope of success. Among the most important are the following, most of which were suggested by Secretary-General Boutros-Ghali in *An Agenda for Peace*:

Public Warning—A Security Council resolution warning of the danger to peace in a situation, calling on the parties to exercise restraint and making clear that the Council will remain seized of the problem, can sometimes have a calming effect. As noted earlier, such action was lacking prior to the Argentine invasion of the Falkland Islands and the Iraqi invasion of Kuwait.

Fact-Finding Missions—The dispatch of a fact-finding team or individual can add to the credibility of a warning resolution and, at the same time, provide a basis for further Council action. Such a mission can also serve to halt the process of escalation and provide, like discussion in the Security Council, a cooling off period for the parties in dispute. Secretary-General Boutros-Ghali sent fact-finding emissaries to several of the new states in the former Soviet Union that faced the possibility of internal conflict, involving in some cases disputes with a neighboring state. The results were favorable if hardly decisive.

Designation of a Special Representative—The Council can call on the Secretary-General to extend his good offices, or appoint a special representative, to assist the parties in resolving their dispute. This would not, in principle, require the prior consent of the parties but their cooperation would obviously be essential.

Referral to the International Court of Justice—In conjunction with one or both of the above measures, the Council can, in an interstate dispute, urge the parties to refer their dispute to the International Court of Justice for adjudication.

Demilitarized Zones—In instances of tension and distrust between neighboring states, the Council can suggest, as a confidence-building measure, the establishment of demilitarized areas along both sides of the border. If the parties agree, the Council can dispatch an observer mission to monitor the area to give further assurance to both parties against surprise attack. If such action is taken in conjunction with the designation of a special representative it can improve the atmosphere for the latter's efforts.

Provision of Humanitarian and Economic Assistance—If peace is threatened by an internal dispute that derives from economic or social causes, the Security Council should be able to call on the Secretary-General to mobilize resources from the UN system (and possibly from member states) that can be quickly applied to alleviate the situation. This would be a new departure for the Security Council, constituting a form of peacebuilding for preventive purposes. This subject is discussed in greater detail in Chapter 6.

These measures have been described in terms of the Security Council. This is not intended to exclude the General Assembly as a source of leverage in preventing conflict. The Assembly can, if it is in session, adopt appropriate warning resolutions and call on the parties to refer their dispute to the International Court of Justice, thus mobilizing public opinion and government support in behalf of a peaceful resolution of a dispute.[7] If, in a situation of internal tension, assistance is needed in organizing an election, or monitoring the vote, the Assembly is the logical body to call on the Secretary-General to provide it. The special office in the Secretariat to give such assistance was established at the Assembly's request. In assessing the prospect of preventive action by the General Assembly, however, it is well to keep in mind that the end of the Cold War did not alter the orientation of the Assembly to the same extent that it did that of the Security Council. Elimination of the division between East and West did little to lessen the division between North and South. Dominated, as it is, by Third World countries, many members of the Assembly are concerned lest UN preventive action infringe on the sovereignty of a small country. The Assembly can therefore be expected to act with caution, if at all, in calling for preventive measures in the case of internal conflict, or in pressing a member state to accept them. The relationship between the Security Council and the Assembly in dealing with threats of internal conflict or humanitarian crises is sensitive and still in need of definition.

INSTRUMENTS FOR DETERRENCE

A fourth element that can be important in the prevention of conflict is the availability of a *deterrence instrumentality*. The United Nations has such an instrumentality in the form of peace-keeping forces (including military observer missions) that can be deployed to decrease the likelihood of both interstate and intrastate conflict. A peace-keeping force was deployed for the first time for strictly deterrent purposes in Macedonia at the beginning of 1993. This subject is pursued in the following chapters on the use of military force by the United Nations for peaceful purposes.

WHY PREVENTION CAN FAIL

The cooperative relationship that developed among the permanent members of the Security Council, particularly between Russia and the United States, as the Cold War came to an end unquestionably enhanced the potential of the United Nations in the prevention of conflict. The mere fact that there was no division between East and West—that in a given dispute the United States was not on one side and the Soviet Union on the other—added to the influence, or leverage, that the Council could exert. Unity in the Council has also increased the credibility of the Secretary-General as a peacemaker. Yet, the United Nations was not able to prevent the deplorable conflicts in Croatia and Bosnia. Why not?

First of all, several of the requirements of conflict prevention that have been described earlier were not yet in place. There was no early warning mechanism in the Secretariat at the time Yugoslavia disintegrated. There was no planning staff to explore options for UN action and to examine the appropriate and realistic roles for the UN and European regional organizations, nor was an effective liaison arrangement between them in existence. More importantly, the concepts of the utilization of peacekeeping for deterrence and for peace-enforcement had not yet been accepted in the United Nations. The UN was unprepared for the disaster.

When conflict first occurred in Croatia at the time of its declaration of independence and the Croats and rebellious Serbs reached cease-fires but did not comply with them, the UN, holding to the traditional concept of peacekeeping, refused to send peacekeepers to enforce compliance. When a large peace-keeping force was subsequently deployed in Croatia after much loss of life and destruction of property, it was given a mandate that could only be successfully implemented by the application of force, which the peacekeepers were not authorized or equipped to use. Peacekeeping, then, was an insufficiently credible instrumentality to establish the necessary conditions for lasting peace in Croatia or to deter the subsequent outbreak of war in Bosnia.

Another factor at the time of the dissolution of Yugoslavia was the untested capability of the regional organizations and the lack of clarity as to the roles that they and the United Nations could most usefully play. Pride of place was given first to the regional organizations which delayed somewhat the focused intervention of the United Nations.

The Croatian experience offered these lessons to the United Nations, lessons clearly reflected in the recommendations contained in Boutros-

Ghali's *An Agenda for Peace*. Steps have been taken to establish an early warning mechanism, clarification and enhancement of the relationship between regional organizations and the UN is being pursued, and the concepts of the deterrent utilization of peacekeeping and of peace-enforcement have become realities. The deployment of peacekeepers to Macedonia to deter external intervention can be seen as a first fruit of the combination of the post–Cold War consensus in the Security Council and the availability of new instrumentalities for deterrence.

Having recorded these positive developments that offer hope of greater UN effectiveness in preventing conflict, it must be added that in the case of Bosnia, there was advance warning of possible catastrophe, with prescient analysis from the Secretary-General's envoy in Yugoslavia. Cyrus Vance informed Secretary-General Pérez de Cuéllar that international recognition of Croatia and its admission to the United Nations before a resolution was found for the overall problem of Yugoslavia would inevitably lead to a declaration of independence by Bosnia and civil war there. The Secretary-General spoke with the permanent members of the Security Council and found that there was no inclination toward a precipitate recognition of Croatia. The United States, in particular, shared the Secretary-General's view that recognition was undesirable at that point. Realizing that the pressure for recognition came from the German Government (which was not on the Security Council) Pérez de Cuéllar wrote directly to German Foreign Minister Genscher and, in what for him were unusually brusque terms, warned that recognition of Croatia (and Slovenia) could do incalculable harm. Genscher replied to the effect that this was not the Secretary-General's business. Pérez de Cuéllar nonetheless sent a further letter warning against recognition of the two newly declared independent countries. This preventive diplomacy was to no avail. Recognition of Croatia and Slovenia followed quickly under German pressure, as did their admission as full members of the United Nations.

This history is recounted here to illustrate that there can be factors affecting the likelihood of conflict that are outside the capacity of even an invigorated United Nations to control. Nevertheless, in a time of a broad commonality of interests among the permanent members of the Security Council (one of which is the prevention or resolution of regional conflict), and of preventive measures newly developed or newly applicable, the United Nations can be a very effective force in preventing conflict. To ensure this, the credibility of the preventive measures must be maintained. Any potential aggressor must be convinced of the capacity of the UN to respond. Any disaffected element in a society threatened by social violence must be convinced that the United Nations has access to resources that can alleviate the causes of tension. Forces deployed in the field by the United Nations must be adequately mandated, equipped and financed to accomplish the objectives expected of them. In the final analysis, the effectiveness of the United Nations in preventing conflict will be determined most of all by the credibility of the Security Council and of the preventive measures at its disposal.

NOTES

1. Javier Pérez de Cuéllar, *Anarchy or Order* (New York: United Nations, 1991), p. 228.

2. Interviews with Niconor Costa-Mendez and Sir Anthony Parsons, UN Oral History Collection, Yale University Library.

3. Unpublished interview with Javier Pérez de Cuéllar.

4. GA Resolution 47/120.

5. UN Charter, Article 65.

6. A description of the various fact-finding and mediation panels established in the past may be found in General Assembly document A/10289, 20 October 1975.

7. The first UN peace-keeping operation, the UN emergency Force in the Sinai, was authorized in 1956 by the General Assembly, Security Council action having been blocked by British and French vetoes. It is now generally accepted, however, that only the Security Council can authorize the deployment of peace-keeping forces.

3

Military Force in the Service of Peace: Peacekeeping in Intrastate Conflict

To maintain peace by military force may seem at first glance—and even second glance—an oxymoron. The term "peace-enforcement" suffers from the same problem. Yet, a primary element in the concept of collective security on which the United Nations is based is that military force will be used, if necessary, to maintain peace and international security. As the meaning of international security has broadened, and as conflict has become increasingly intrastate in character, the purposes for which the application of military force may be needed in one form or another have also become more varied. This is amply evidenced by the recent UN, or UN-authorized operations in Namibia, Central America, the Persian Gulf, Cambodia, Yugoslavia, Somalia and elsewhere. In the post–Cold War era, the use of military personnel (together frequently with police and civilian personnel) has assumed new dimensions and new potential, owing in large part to the prevalence of intrastate conflict. This has raised many questions both for the UN and for member states regarding the dangers of expanded military deployment, of the adequacy of resources and the procedures for command and control, and of the possible infringement of national sovereignty.

A HISTORY OF DOMESTIC INVOLVEMENT

The purpose of UN peace-keeping forces has traditionally been understood as that of interpositioning, with the consent of the parties concerned, between two hostile forces after a truce or cease-fire has been achieved to discourage a resumption of hostilities. From the beginning, however, the purpose went beyond that. In the first full-fledged peace-keeping operation mounted as a result of the Suez War in 1956, the original purpose was to "secure and supervise the cessation of hostilities in accordance with the aforementioned resolution" (which included the withdrawal of foreign forces from Egyptian territory).[1] This was expanded, or interpreted, in accordance with subsequent General Assembly resolutions, to include deployment in the Gaza Strip to maintain quiet during and after the withdrawal of Israeli forces and to prevent illegal crossings of the armistice line by civilians of either side. Notably, the United Nations Emergency Force (UNEF) was expected to assume responsibility for the civil administration of the Gaza Strip and did so for a brief period.

In the ensuing years, peacekeeping has encompassed such varied functions as to make definition difficult. To appreciate the role that peacekeeping can play in intrastate conflicts it is useful to examine the ways in which six diverse UN peace-keeping operations were involved in the domestic concerns of the countries where they were deployed: the Congo, Cyprus, southern Lebanon, Namibia, Nicaragua and Haiti. (Haiti was not originally designated a peace-keeping operation by the UN.)

The Congo

A United Nations peace-keeping force (ONUC) was sent to the Congo essentially to stabilize conditions that had become chaotic and violent when the country gained independence from Belgium. The new government requested UN military assistance "to protect the national territory of the Congo against the present external aggression which is a threat to international peace."[2] There was no request to restore internal stability. However, Secretary-General Hammarskjöld recommended to the Security Council the establishment of a peace-keeping force to assist the government of the Congo in maintaining law and order until, with technical assistance from the UN, the Congolese national security forces were able to meet these tasks. The Security Council authorized the Secretary-General to take the necessary steps for this purpose and called on Belgium to withdraw its troops from the territory.[3] Thus began what, until the operation in Cambodia, was the largest UN peace-keeping operation (reaching a peak of 20,000 troops plus a large civilian corps) and one with a profound influence on internal developments in a member state.[4]

The Secretary-General was fully aware of the sensitivity of the action that the UN was undertaking in the Congo, both in terms of the attitudes of the foreign countries having a strong interest in the course of events in the Congo, and of the resistance of the Congolese government to any seeming challenge to its authority within the country, even though such authority was highly tenuous. In his first report to the Security Council on the Congo operation,[5] Hammarskjöld stated the principles that would govern the activities of ONUC, among which were the following:

> Although dispatched at the request of the Congolese Government, and although it might be considered as serving as an arm of the Government for the purpose of the maintenance of law and order and protection of life, the Force was necessarily under the exclusive command of the United Nations. The Force is thus not under the orders of the Congolese Government and cannot be permitted *to become a party to any internal conflict* (Emphasis added).
>
> The authority of the United Nations Force may not be exercised within the Congo either in competition with the representatives of its government or in co-operation with them in any joint operation. The United Nations operation must be separate and distinct from activities by any national authorities.
>
> The Force cannot be used to enforce any specific political solution of pending problems or to influence the political balance decisive for such a solution.
>
> The United Nations military units are not authorized to use force except in self-defense. They are never to take the initiative in the use of force, but are entitled to respond with force to an attack with arms, including attacks intended to make them withdraw from positions they occupied under orders of the Force Commander.

Each of these principles was severely tested during the Congo operation and, in some instances, rather elastically interpreted. Patrice Lumumba, the first prime minister of the Congo, never understood or accepted that the UN force could not be used in collaboration with Congolese troops to end the secession of Katanga; the failure of Hammarskjöld to use the UN Force for this purpose was a major factor in the withdrawal by the USSR of confidence in the Secretary-General.

The principle of non-use of force was equally difficult to apply and eventually had to be modified. For one thing, commanders in the field, unused to the subtleties of UN language, did not know how to interpret the principle in practice. In visits to the Congo, the Secretary-General's military advisor found the commanders confused. He sought to clarify for them individually how the principle was to be interpreted.[6]

In light of the deteriorating security situation in the Congo the Security Council on February 21, 1961, adopted a resolution authorizing the use of force, if necessary as a last resort, to prevent civil war in the Congo.[7] Hammarskjöld was not entirely happy with this resolution, as it did not provide "a wider legal basis" for action;[8] nonetheless, on the basis of this

resolution UN forces took military action in Katanga that contributed
decisively to ending its secession and that could be seen as at odds with the
principle enunciated earlier by Hammarskjöld (and approved by the Security Council), i.e., that the UN Force could not be used to enforce any specific
political solution of pending problems or become party to any internal
conflict.

Simultaneously with efforts to maintain security and law and order in
the Congo, the UN Force (primarily through its civilian component)
undertook to assure the continuation of essential services, to restore and
organize the administrative machinery of government, and to train the
Congolese to run the machinery.[9] For these purposes UN staff members
were placed in the government ministries and in provincial offices as well
as in infrastructure operational facilities. Certain police responsibilities
were carried out. The representative of the Secretary-General even exercised authority over the functioning of the Leopoldville airport and of
the Leopoldville radio (which was interpreted by some as contrary to
the principle of not taking sides in internal conflicts enunciated by
Hammarskjöld).

Although a major concern of Dag Hammarskjöld in recommending UN
action in the Congo was the possibility that the situation there could bring
the USA and the USSR into direct conflict, the resolution authorizing the
deployment of the peace-keeping force makes no reference to the danger
that the situation posed to international security. The Security Council
called for the withdrawal of Belgian troops but the objectives established
for the peace-keeping force were internal. No reservations were expressed
that the action might be contrary to Article 2 of the Charter, possibly because
the Belgian military intervention lent a clear international dimension to the
crisis. Nonetheless, it can hardly be contested that the Congo operation was
undertaken to deal with an intrastate situation. The operation revealed the
serious—even fatal—problems that such an operation can entail, especially
when undertaken within an environment of hostility and mistrust between
the United States and the former Soviet Union.

The problems were not only those related to the UN role in the conflicts
between the various Congolese factions and in the Katanga secession. There
were also problems that derived from the capability of the UN to perform
a task of such size and complexity. Given the number of troops required,
some inevitably were inadequately trained or prepared for peace-keeping
duties. Some senior military officers were incompetent, and some senior
civilian personnel showed mistaken judgement. The internal nature of the
situation with which the UN was dealing brought the Secretary-General
under harsh attack, with serious implications for his continued effectiveness in leading the organization had he lived. A financial strain was placed
on the UN that was to trouble the organization for many years. The attitude

of many UN members toward the UN Congo operation has long been "never again."

Yet, with the perspective of thirty years, the UN Congo operation must be viewed as a success and one with positive implications for the role of the UN in dealing now and in the future with intrastate conflicts. Internal stability was restored; the territorial integrity of a newly decolonized country was maintained; the danger of East-West confrontation was avoided; and the UN proved its capacity—even if imperfect—to mount a large operation and to carry it through in an environment of domestic violence and, at times, hostility toward the UN, itself.

The principles formulated by Hammarskjöld with reference to the Congo were intended to ensure the complete impartiality of the UN peacekeeping force and to avoid any conflict with the provision in the UN Charter prohibiting intervention in the domestic affairs of states. They could hardly be formulated otherwise today. Yet, in practice, it now proves even less practical than then to comply strictly with such principles and still hope to achieve an end to internal conflict.

Cyprus

In the face of the violent conflict that had broken out between the Greek and the Turkish Cypriot communities in Cyprus the Security Council, at the request of the governments of Cyprus and the United Kingdom, decided in March 1964 that a UN peace-keeping force should be sent to the island. In the resolution that was adopted,[10] it was noted that the situation in Cyprus was likely to endanger international peace and security. But the mandate that was given to the Force (UNFICYP) pertained entirely to the intrastate conflict. Specifically, the force was to prevent a recurrence of fighting between the communities and to contribute to the maintenance and restoration of law and order and a return to normal conditions. This has remained UNFICYP's core mandate to the present day, even though it has had to be exercised under the vastly changed conditions that resulted from the 1974 coup d'état, the subsequent Turkish invasion and the effective partitioning of the island.

As in the case of the Congo, the Secretary-General (at this time U Thant) recommended, and the Security Council approved, notably similar principles that were to guide the activities of UNFICYP,[11] among which were the following:

- The Force must be under the exclusive control and command of the United Nations at all times.
- The Force will undertake no functions inconsistent with the provisions of the Security Council resolution.

- The Force is to use arms only for self-defense in the interest of preserving international peace and security, of preventing a recurrence of fighting and of contributing to the maintenance and restoration of law and order and normal conditions.
- The personnel of the Force must act with restraint and complete impartiality toward the Greek and Turkish Cypriot communities.

With the Congo experience no doubt in mind, Secretary-General U Thant, in his report to the Security Council, made a special effort to clarify how "self-defense" was to be interpreted. Self-defense, he said, includes the defense of UN posts, premises and vehicles under armed attack, as well as the support of other UNFICYP personnel under armed attack. "Examples in which troops may be authorized to use force include attempts by force to compel them to withdraw from a position which they occupy under orders from their commanders, attempts by force to disarm them, and attempts by force to prevent them from carrying out their responsibilities as ordered by their commanders." The self-defense, of course, would be against hostile *domestic* forces under the UNFICYP mandate. A very similar definition of self-defense is applied today in the UN peace-keeping operation in Bosnia-Herzegovina.

Given the nature of its mandate "to contribute to the maintenance and restoration of law and order and a return to normal conditions," UNFICYP was established with a civilian police component (UNCIVPOL). Among the duties defined by the Secretary-General for this police force was the investigation of incidents where Greek and Turkish Cypriots were involved with the opposite community, including searches for persons reported as missing. At a later stage, after the Turkish invasion in 1974, it was agreed that UNFICYP would be responsible for all security and police functions in mixed villages.

In fact, both the military and civilian components of UNFICYP have been directly involved in what normally would be considered the functions of the domestic authorities, whether national or municipal. It can hardly be otherwise in any situation in which a UN peace-keeping force has the responsibility of preventing a recurrence of conflict and maintaining law and order among hostile elements of a national society. Moreover, restoration of law and order and a return to normal conditions have entailed extensive humanitarian and logistic assistance by UNFICYP. Electric power in the northern part of the island is supplied from the southern part. Water sources flow across the cease-fire lines and sometimes crisscross the buffer zone. Assistance is provided to Greek Cypriots and Maronites in the north and Turkish Cypriots in the south including medical evacuation when needed. After the landing of Turkish troops in 1974, the humanitarian needs were so great that a special humanitarian and economics branch was set up at UNFICYP headquarters. With as many as one third of the island's population displaced, however, humanitarian needs were beyond the capacity of the peace-keeping operation, and the UN High Commissioner for Refugees was designated as coordinator of UN humanitarian assistance for Cyprus, thus enlisting a separate UN office in meeting responsibilities assumed by the UN as part of peacekeeping.

Since the Turkish invasion, UNFICYP has been, in effect, the administering authority in the buffer zone established between the forces on the two sides in 1974. This covers three percent of the island and includes some of its most valuable agricultural land. According to the December 7, 1990, report of a Secretariat Review Team on the United Nations Peacekeeping Force in Cyprus:

> There is no formal agreement between UNFICYP and the two sides on the complete delineation of the buffer zone. As a result, UNFICYP finds itself supervising, by loose mutual consent, two constantly disputed cease-fire lines. . . . In addition to its constant endeavors to maintain the military *status quo* UNFICYP must also preserve the integrity of the buffer zone from unauthorized entry or activities by civilians. As a result, UNFICYP has become increasingly involved in crowd control. . . . While the primary responsibility for preventing demonstrators from crossing the cease-fire line rests with the civilian authorities concerned, UNFICYP troops and UNCIVPOL . . . must prevent demonstrators from entering the buffer zone. . . . Farming permits are issued [by UNFICYP] to proven owners of land. . . . To take into account the security requirements of the two sides as well as the safety of the farmers, UNFICYP has drawn up farming security lines to delimit the farming area within the buffer zone. . . . In areas that have proven to be contentious, farmers from either community are escorted by UNFICYP troops on a daily basis. . . . UNFICYP must keep the farming area under constant supervision from observation posts or through patrols.[12]

If a crime is committed in the buffer zone it is an open question who has the authority to arrest.

Today, thirty years after its deployment, UNFICYP is taken for granted by both sides in Cyprus. The author had the opportunity to meet in April 1991 with the UNFICYP Force Commander and members of both his military and civilian staff, to observe UNFICYP operations and to talk with senior officials on both the Greek Cypriot and Turkish Cypriot sides. UNFICYP activities that touch on the domestic administration of the island have not led to any appreciable resentment or resistance on the part of local authorities, although the Cyprus Government is sensitive to any implied derogation of its territorial sovereignty. The only complaint voiced in the Foreign Ministry of Cyprus pertained to the issuance of passes by UNFICYP for entry to the buffer zone. The Ministry took exception to this practice as inappropriate since this was a function of the sovereign government; but this was not portrayed as a serious issue. Interestingly, the only major complaint stated by senior representatives on both the Greek Cypriot and Turkish Cypriot sides was that the United Nations should have from the beginning been more aggressive in *enforcing* peace on the island. The peace-keeping operation was viewed in this perspective as misguided and ineffective although no one suggested that within the limits of its mandate UNFICYP had not been extremely useful, even essential to the security and well-being of the island. And, of course, the two sides have sharply conflicting views as to what regime the UN should have enforced to bring peace.

UNFICYP has never had a peace-making mandate. This function rests with the Secretary-General and his Special Representative for Cyprus. It might have been expected, however, that the extensive UNFICYP humanitarian activities would have brought some conciliation, at least at the local level, between the two sides. This has not been the case. UNFICYP has facilitated the peace-making process by stabilizing the security situation on the island without which the political efforts to resolve the Cyprus problem—unproductive as they have been—could not have gone forward. On the other hand, it cannot be said that peacekeeping in this case has contributed to bringing the two sides together or to building an improved basis for peace.

Southern Lebanon

The United Nations Interim Force in Lebanon (UNIFIL) was deployed in March 1978 in immediate response to the invasion of southern Lebanon by Israel. To appreciate the responsibilities it was given and the role it plays even today, however, the deployment of the Force must be seen in the larger context of the civil war that had engulfed Lebanon in 1975. As a result of that war and the expansion of control by the Palestine Liberation Organization (PLO) in the south, the Lebanese government was unable to exercise its authority south of the Litani river, the area invaded by Israel. Therefore, UNIFIL was deployed into an area where the national government did not govern, where a foreign army was in the field and where a number of local authorities vied for control. It is hardly surprising under the circumstances that the mandate defined for UNIFIL was less than clear. Patently it would have to operate within a complex domestic environment as it has, now, for sixteen years.

The Security Council, in authorizing the deployment of UNIFIL, stated three purposes for the Force:[13]

- confirm the withdrawal of Israeli forces;
- restore international peace and security;
- assist the Lebanese Government to restore its authority in the area.

The Secretary-General, Kurt Waldheim, defined, as in previous peace-keeping undertakings, terms of reference for UNIFIL, terms that had to take account of the internal role that was to be played. Among the provisions were the following:

- the Force would establish and maintain itself in an "area of operation" to be defined in light of the tasks set by the Security Council;
- it would seek to prevent the recurrence of fighting;
- it would ensure that its area of operation would not be used for hostile activities of any kind;
- once the withdrawal of Israeli forces from Lebanese territory was confirmed, it would control movement in the area and take all necessary measures to restore the authority of the Lebanese Government.

In stating these principles, the Secretary-General placed particular emphasis on the non-use of force and nonintervention in the internal affairs of the host country. UNIFIL must not take on responsibilities that fell under the government of the country in which it was operating.[14]

It was never possible to agree with the parties concerned on an official definition of the area in which UNIFIL was to operate. As Israeli forces withdrew from southern Lebanon, UNIFIL established itself in the area except in an enclave considered by Israel to be particularly sensitive in terms of PLO infiltration. There a militia under the command of Lebanese Major Haddad, termed by the UN *"de facto"* forces, took over and refused to allow UNIFIL to deploy, thus enormously complicating UNIFIL's task. These forces, supported and directed by Israel and Israeli military personnel, continued their presence in this area, sometimes moving also into the area of UN deployment.

The principles for the operation defined by the Secretary-General entailed an inherent contradiction. The UN Force was not to take on the responsibilities of the Lebanese Government, but in reality the Lebanese Government was not able to exercise its authority in the area. The task of assisting the Lebanese Government to restore its authority inevitably involved undertaking activities that would normally be the responsibility of the government in Beirut, until the government was able to do so.

Looking to the future functioning of UN peacekeeping, it is of some importance to consider what UNIFIL has accomplished given the restrictions in its mandate and the extraordinarily complex circumstances in which it must operate. Taking the purposes defined for it by the Security Council, which despite changing circumstances have not been materially altered, how far has it progressed toward accomplishing them?

The first was to confirm the withdrawal of Israeli forces from Lebanese territory, a traditional function of UN peacekeeping in cases of interstate conflict. But in Lebanon the objective of bringing about the withdrawal of foreign forces assumed an intrastate dimension when the Israeli forces were replaced in important respects by the internal *de facto* forces (now called the South Lebanon Army). UNIFIL was neither mandated nor equipped to do battle with this surrogate force, even though the force prevented the full deployment of UNIFIL and at times attacked UNIFIL posts. (The use of force by UNIFIL has never been authorized in southern Lebanon as it was in the Congo.)

The second purpose was restoring international peace and security in the area. International peace and security were and still are affected by violence and conflict in Lebanon. The extensive presence of Syrian forces in the country and the two Israeli invasions, in particular, have given a clear interstate dimension to the conflict. Yet, aside from confirming the withdrawal of Israeli forces, UNIFIL was not in a position to influence the larger *international* factors in the security situation in its area of operation. When the second Israeli invasion occurred, traversing in the process the area of UN deployment, UNIFIL could not stop it or even delay it very long. In reality what UNIFIL has been concerned with is *internal* security, and in this it has been quite effective. It has prevented the passage of "armed elements" through the area of operation, initially with less than 100 percent effectiveness (due in part to extensive hidden arms caches in the area that PLO elements could retrieve after entering the area), but eventually with a high rate of success.

It has been a more difficult, if less hazardous, task to enhance the security of the inhabitants of the area—to protect them from the encroachment and pressures of internal elements and to do so without the powers of arrest or punishment. UNIFIL has done this in the first instance through the benevolent influence of its sheer presence. Its patrols have given continuing physical evidence of this. Force members have established and maintained contact with village leaders. UNIFIL has repeatedly sought to curb attacks by the South Lebanon Army on villages within the area of operation and to prevent the entrenchment in the area of armed PLO elements. The physical presence of UNIFIL battalion outposts has afforded a sense of security evidenced by the impressive revival of villages located in their immediate vicinity. Compared to other areas in Lebanon, the entire UNIFIL area of operation is notable for its economic health, its new construction and the rehabilitation of extensive farm land, although new destruction occurred during a fierce Israeli bombardment of Islamic fundamentalist centers in 1993.

UNIFIL *has* undertaken responsibilities normally belonging to the host government or local authorities. In particular it has controlled movement *within* Lebanon. It has performed police functions, receiving reports of civil offenses and turning them over to the most appropriate local authority available. In the earlier years after its deployment, UNIFIL participated actively in the restoration of essential services and in the rebuilding of houses, schools and roads. Yet UNIFIL has never administered the area. It has drawn and maintained a careful line in this regard and in the process shown that a peace-keeping force can have a significant—and beneficial— influence on an internal situation without having a mandate to administer.

The third purpose for which UNIFIL was deployed was to assist the government of Lebanon in the restoration of its authority in the area. There are two ways in which UNIFIL has gone about this mandate. One is through the stabilization process just described, in which in the period prior to the second Israeli invasion, UNIFIL cooperated with gendarmes remaining in the area and thus assisted an arm of the Lebanese Government to exercise authority in the maintenance of law and order. By limiting the presence of forces hostile to the reassertion of the Lebanese Government's authority in the area, that is the *de facto* forces in particular, UNIFIL contributed to a more hospitable environment in the area for the restoration of Lebanese authority. Finally, again prior to 1982, UNIFIL made it possible for elements of the Lebanese Army that were able to reach the UNIFIL area of operation to be stationed with UNIFIL units. When Israel occupied the area after the 1982 invasion, all evidence of the central government's authority disappeared. Now, again, the Lebanese Army is present in several of the villages in the area, but they have returned without any direct assistance from UNIFIL.

The situation in southern Lebanon poses a problem for peace-keepers that may well be present in other intrastate conflicts. UNIFIL was clearly deployed in support of the legitimate Lebanese Government. Insofar as its mandate pertained to the external aspects of the problem—the presence of foreign forces—its desirable course of action was clear: to get the foreign troops out by observation, persuasion and agreement on the withdrawal process. But how, in a situation of civil war, can a UN force act in behalf of the government when there are local elements that are hostile to the return of central control? Today the South Lebanon Army exercises military con- trol in southern Lebanon except in the UNIFIL area, and even there its influence is not unfelt. A "Civil Administration" has been created, also under strong Israeli influence, that functions as a kind of civilian arm of the South Lebanon Army. The village authorities welcome the presence of gendarmes but tend to doubt their protective capacity. They contend that, even if the Lebanese Army should be deployed in Southern Lebanon, the United Nations should stay. The question of principle that emerges from this situation is: when a peace-keeping force has been deployed at the request of a legitimate government, how far should the force go in assisting the government to overcome domestic opposition to its authority?

This is the question that arose in an even more intense form in the Congo. At that time the Secretary-General took the position that the secession of

Katanga was essentially an internal matter and that the UN Force should not be used to support the central government in bringing the secession to an end by military means. But in the end it did. In Lebanon a specific purpose of the UN deployment was to assist the government in restoring its authority. This, until now, has proved largely impossible.

Namibia

The mandate of the UN peace-keeping operation with regard to Namibia (UNTAG—the United Nations Transitional Assistance Group) was the most far-reaching and the most internally oriented ever given to a peace-keeping undertaking prior to the operations in Cambodia and Somalia. In terms of international law, full responsibility for Namibia reverted to the United Nations (as successor to the League of Nations) following termination by the General Assembly in 1966 of South Africa's mandate to administer the Territory of South West Africa. Therefore the UNTAG mandate could not be construed as authorizing intervention by the United Nations in the domestic affairs of a sovereign state. However, an allegedly independent government was in place and, under the terms of the settlement agreement incorporated in Security Council resolution 435 (1978), South Africa was authorized to administer through an Administrator-General the elections that would be the key to Namibia's independence. So, in reality, UNTAG had responsibilities directly affecting the security and administration of Namibia, but actual authority to administer the territory rested with a local government and, for the elections, with South Africa.

While military personnel were the largest element in UNTAG, its central purpose was political, namely, to establish conditions for the holding of free, universal elections in Namibia and to ensure that they were carried out in acceptable fashion. All of its responsibilities related to this central objective. These included

- Monitoring the cease-fire between SWAPO and South African forces.
- Monitoring the reduction and eventual removal of South African forces from Namibia and the return to civilian status in Namibia of SWAPO guerrillas.
- Monitoring the borders to prevent infiltration.
- Arranging for the release of political prisoners and the return of Namibians living in exile.
- Ensuring that the remaining South African-organized security forces (SWAPOL) carried out their duties in a manner consistent with free and fair elections.

- Bringing about political and legal changes as necessary conditions for such elections and for the introduction of democratic government in a newly independent country.

The civilian and police (CIVPOL) elements of UNTAG became intimately involved in political developments and in the maintenance of security in the territory. Forty-two political offices were established throughout Namibia to work with the local administrative authorities in ensuring that the essential political processes took place. In many instances they performed a *conciliation* function by bringing black and white elements of the population together for meetings where they could discuss the stake that they shared in the successful transition of their country to independence.

CIVPOL's primary function was to monitor the South West African Police so that it would carry out its duty of maintaining law and order in an efficient and nonpartisan way. CIVPOL had no powers of arrest and could, in principle, influence the standard of policing only indirectly. Yet in the course of events, it often patrolled on its own and was frequently present at political meetings when the local police authorities were not. The UN police function proved to be especially important in Namibia, and CIVPOL's size had to be increased during the operation, whereas the military element of UNTAG was scaled down in size from original estimates and never reached even its scaled down numbers.

Perhaps the most enduring UN influence on the domestic development of Namibia resulted from the legal advice given by UNTAG on the repeal of discriminatory legislation, on the enactment of legislation governing the elections and on the drafting of the country's constitution. Many changes in the legislation and in the constitution were made at UNTAG's insistence. The UN was intimately involved in both the political process leading to the elections and in supervising the entire electoral process. The Secretary-General himself, during a visit to Namibia in July 1989, convened a meeting of all the political parties taking part in the elections and suggested that they meet regularly with the Special Representative to resolve any problems that might arise. The Special Representative subsequently worked out with the parties a political Code of Conduct that defined ground rules with which they voluntarily complied in their election campaigning.

Thus the UN peace-keeping operation in Namibia, which technically had neither enforcement nor administrative authority, actually performed a wide spectrum of functions that normally are within the responsibility of the national or local government. UNTAG controlled the borders; influenced the internal political process (without favoring any one political party); contributed to the maintenance of law and order and supervised the local police force; facilitated the return and resettlement of exiles; kept the population informed of developments through an active information program; and did much to determine the constitutional regime under which

Namibia would be governed. As the UN itself has stated, UNTAG was deeply involved in the whole political process (which means the domestic process) of Namibia's transition from illegally occupied colony to sovereign and independent state.[15]

Nicaragua

As part of the Central American Peace Process the United Nations undertook three distinct actions with regard to Nicaragua. Together they can be seen as a major peace-keeping operation that involved the United Nations very directly in domestic developments in a member state.[16]

The first operation to be undertaken, in November 1989, was the United Nations Observer Group in Central American (ONUCA), which was established by the Security Council.[17] Its mandate was a) to verify the cessation of aid to irregular forces and insurrectionist movements; and b) to verify the non-use of the territory of one state for attacks on other states. Consisting of unarmed military observers who carried out regular patrols by land vehicles, helicopters and patrol boats, ONUCA would seem to be in the "classical" peace-keeping tradition of border observation. But significantly, ONUCA was not intended to prevent infiltration by national forces, but rather by "irregular forces and insurrectionist movements," that is, persons, who for the most part were nationals of the country into which they would be infiltrating. Moreover, verification that the territory of one state is not being utilized for attacks on other states clearly involves intervention within the borders of sovereign states. (The only comparable undertaking in UN peace-keeping history is the prevention of the transit of armed elements through the UN area of operations in southern Lebanon.) The present relevance of the potential infiltration of Bosnian-born Serb fighters into Bosnia from Serbia is evident.

The second UN operation with regard to Nicaragua was the International Support and Verification Commission (CIAV), the purpose of which was to make possible the voluntary demobilization, repatriation or relocation in Nicaragua or third countries of the members of the Nicaraguan resistance and their families. The functions of CIAV, as stated in a Joint Plan agreed upon by the presidents of the five Central American countries, included good offices, disarmament and the custody of weapons, humanitarian assistance and development aid. CIAV was established by joint decision of the Secretaries-General of the UN and of the OAS; but in reporting to the Security Council, Secretary-General Pérez de Cuéllar noted that demobilization concerned the Council "since it is an operation of a clearly military nature. . . . This is not a task which can be taken on by civilian personnel of the United Nations. . . . This task should be entrusted to military units equipped with defensive weapons. The launching of such an operation is clearly within the competence of the Security Council."[18] Subsequently, the Security Council did authorize the use of such a military force, which was provided by Venezuela.

The monitoring of the national elections, held on February 25, 1991, was the third responsibility with regard to Nicaragua undertaken by the United Nations. The United Nations Observer Mission for the Verification of the Elections in Nicaragua (ONUVEN) was established by the Secretary-General in response to a request from the Nicaraguan Minister for Foreign Affairs. The Secretary-General acted within the terms of the General Assembly's earlier resolution calling on him to afford the fullest possible support to the peace process in Central America.[19] The mandate of ONUVEN went well beyond observing the elections. It included

- verification that political parties were equitably represented in the Supreme Electoral Council;
- verification that political parties enjoyed complete freedom of organization and mobilization;
- verification that all political parties had equitable access to state television and radio;
- verification that electoral rolls were properly drawn up.

Thus ONUVEN undertook the job of ensuring that the conditions within which the election campaign and the elections took place were satisfactory for free and fair elections. This went far beyond observing and reporting on the elections.

Technically, ONUVEN was not considered a peace-keeping operation since no military personnel were involved. Authorization of the Security Council was thus not required. In reality, however, it was an integral part of the overall UN effort to assist in the resolution of the internal conflict in Nicaragua. This conflict had evident implications for international security and for the peace of the region. There could be little doubt that the UN was acting in accordance with the first principle of the Charter "to bring about by peaceful means, and in conformity with the principles of justice and international law, adjustment or settlement of international disputes *or situations* which might lead to a breach of the peace" (Emphasis added). Yet the direct involvement of the UN in sensitive activities falling normally entirely within the domestic jurisdiction of a country constituted an added dimension to what the UN can do *in* member states in pursuit of this principle.

Haiti

As was the case in Nicaragua, the government of Haiti in 1991 formally requested the United Nations to provide electoral assistance. The provisional government identified the holding of free, fair and credible elections as a matter of top priority in ending the violence and instability that had plagued the country. Interestingly, the first response from the UN, undertaken at the initiative of the Secretary-General, was the dispatch of a technical mission, financed by the United Nations Development Program, to help establish a credible and honest electoral process through technical and practical advice, practical training measures and the exchange of experience with other developing countries. In addition, the Secretary-General appointed a Personal Representative for Haiti and asked him to clarify further the Haitian request. In accordance with the clarifications that were subsequently received, which were communicated by the Secretary-General both to the Security Council and the General Assembly, the General Assembly by consensus[20] asked the Secretary-General to meet the Haitian requests for a) electoral observers, b) two or three security advisors to assist the Haitian Coordinating Committee for the Security of Electoral Activities and c) "specialized observers with solid experience in the field of public order." The result was the establishment of the United Nations Observer Group for the Verification of the Elections in Haiti (ONUVEH).

The role undertaken by the UN in Haiti constituted the first intervention in a member state in which neither decolonization nor an immediate or evident threat to international security was involved. The security in question was internal. The need for the assistance requested by the Haitian Government in this area was compelling. Nevertheless, the introduction of "security" within a clearly internal context was widely seen as significant in terms of UN procedures. A case could be, and was, made by some experts within the Secretariat, that any security issue lay within the competence of the Security Council, especially if military officers were to be involved as was unavoidable in the case of Haiti. However, there was strong resistance among Third World countries, especially in Latin America, to the Security Council acting to authorize election monitoring in Haiti, since they saw in this the danger of affording the Permanent Members a precedent to intervene in the internal affairs of other small countries. Thus it was that the General Assembly took action on a matter involving security. For the record, ONUVEH, like ONUVEN, was not considered a peace-keeping operation, even though military personnel were seconded to Haiti from UN peace-keeping operations elsewhere to serve as security observers. The General Assembly did not authorize funds for ONUVEH and the only available source was a contingency account for urgent needs related to international security. This account had been drawn on in the past largely, if not exclusively, for actions authorized by the Security Council. UN documents relating to the financing of ONUVEH fuzz the relationship between the funds used and international security.

Despite the evident sensitivity, ONUVEH did play an important part in the establishment of domestic conditions favorable for free elections. Responsibility for electoral security lay exclusively with the Haitian armed forces, but the UN advisors established close ties with the Coordinating Committee and participated in all of its preparatory work. They did similar service with local military authorities responsible for drawing up and implementing local security plans. The observers identified sensitive areas with a potential for conflict, and by such action, and their mere presence, stiffened the back of the responsible military authorities. ONUVEH assisted in ensuring coordination and understanding between the Haitian electoral and military authorities. Perhaps the most important of all "domestic" actions taken by ONUVEH was the so-called quick count of votes that it completed immediately after the balloting ended. This projection was so definitive as to the election results that it discouraged any temptation on the part of candidates to challenge the election before the official results were announced a week later.

The United Nations electoral team left Haiti immediately after the electoral process was successfully completed. Unfortunately, the free election of a government after so many years of dictatorship was not sufficient to establish a sound basis for democracy. The freely elected government of President Aristide was quickly overthrown. Having done too little to strengthen democratic institutions, the UN, along with member states, have faced the even more difficult problem of restoring a democratic government. Had a properly mandated UN peace-building mission remained in Haiti to assist in retraining the police, restructuring the military establishment and monitoring respect for human rights, the dark period of military rule might have been avoided.

As matters developed, the United Nations, for the first time in its history, authorized enforcement action under Chapter VII of the Charter in order to restore democratic government in a member state. The Security Council first imposed economic sanctions when those applied by the OAS proved ineffective and then took the historically notable step of authorizing "member states to form a multilateral force under unified command and control and, in this framework, to use all necessary means to facilitate the departure from Haiti of the military leadership, . . . the prompt return of the legitimately elected President and the restoration of the legitimate authorities of the Government of Haiti, and to *establish and maintain a secure and stable environment that will permit implementation of the Governors Island Agreement*" (Emphasis added).[21]

The Security Council further decided that once the multilateral force had terminated its mission, the United Nations Mission in Haiti (UNMIH) would for a period of six months assist the Government of Haiti in fulfilling its responsibilities in connection with sustaining a secure and stable environment and the professionalization of the Haitian armed forces and the creation of a separate police force—exactly what the UN mission had not done following the successful completion of Haiti's first free elections.

In Haiti, the UN acted with the enthusiastic approval of the legitimately elected President of Haiti. This does not lessen the significance, however, of UN enforcement action not only to strengthen democratic institutions and bring an end to the violation of the human rights of the population, but also to restore deemocratic government when it had been overthrown.

PAST EXPERIENCE AS A GUIDE FOR THE FUTURE

As is apparent from the foregoing review, UN peace-keeping operations in situations of intrastate conflict have a long history. They have been successful in stabilizing domestic situations by preventing a renewal of internal armed conflict (Cyprus), strengthening infrastructure (the Congo), improving local security (southern Lebanon) or facilitating an electoral process intended to lead to political stability, a result achieved in Nicaragua and Namibia but, unfortunately, not in Haiti. It has been shown that simply by its presence, the United Nations alters the conditions in which an electoral process takes place and contributes substantially to the success of elections. A Secretariat official who participated in the Haiti operation has observed that the presence of the UN introduces a transparency that has two beneficial consequences: it encourages the authorities charged with organization and the security of the electoral process to meet fully their responsibilities; and at the same time it discourages those who might be tempted to interfere with the electoral process or falsify the results.

While the UN is by no means the only organization that has been requested by governments to observe elections, governments have shown that they attach special value to UN participation as being totally objective and trustworthy. Thus the government of Haiti invited the OAS and a number of nongovernmental organizations as well as the UN to observe its elections, but it requested only the UN to provide security advisers and security observers. This was internally the most sensitive function for a non-Haitian agency to undertake and was of critical importance to the success of the elections.

Through such stabilizing actions, UN peace-keeping operations in domestic conflict situations frequently perform a highly important postconflict, *peace-building* role by reducing the causes of the social tensions that have given rise to conflict within a society. The strengthening of democratic processes, conciliation among population groups, encouragement of respect for human rights (as specifically mandated in El Salvador) and in the alleviation of humanitarian problems are all part of this process. By carrying out such functions in a country seriously threatened by strife before conflict begins, the deployment of peace-keeping forces can also serve a deterrent purpose, enhancing the conflict prevention capacity of the United Nations. In intrastate conflicts the process of peacekeeping can, in itself, be part of a peace-building process. This was already true in the Congo where the UN sought, not always successfully, to bring the various leaders together and, in the end, did contribute to conciliation and the maintenance of national unity. It was true in Namibia where, as we have seen, the functions of the peace-keeping force were central to the establishment of a constitutional system and a freely elected government that promise to be the basis of an internally peaceful country. Moreover, members of the peace-keeping operation in Namibia sought, with success, to conciliate elements within society that had traditionally viewed each other with hostility. In Nicaragua the modalities have been different but the effect quite similar. UN assistance in the electoral process—in the strengthening of democratic procedures—should be seen as part of this peace-building process within domestic societies.

From this survey, it is clear that, when utilized in connection with internal conflict, UN peacekeeping has been most successful when a combination of measures can be applied such as the training of civilian police, the disarmament of contending internal forces and the monitoring of human rights. The preparation and supervision of free elections, while essential elements in the development of a stable society, are not alone sufficient to guarantee an enduring democracy.

This must be taken into account as the UN role in conflict deterrence and peace-building is pursued. Depending on the circumstances in a particular country, a United Nations peace-keeping operation should be equipped, *mutatis mutandi*, to further conciliation between hostile groups, contribute to fair and constructive civil administration, and encourage respect for human rights. To meet such responsibilities, military and civilian peace-keeping personnel need more knowledge and sensitivity concerning the area where they are deployed and its inhabitants than has generally been the case. This again underlines the importance of acquiring extensive information on the political, social and economic circumstances of a situation and of analysis and planning before an intrastate peace-keeping operation is undertaken. Above all, when the UN undertakes through a peace-keeping mission to assist in the holding of free elections and the establishment of a democratic government, it must be prepared to maintain the mission, reconstituted as appropriate, in the country long enough to ensure stabilization of the internal situation and the establishment of those instruments of government needed for the survival of democracy.

If UN personnel are to be involved in elections they need special training on the procedures involved. Some training is given to Secretariat personnel involved in such missions, but no way has yet been developed to give training to the military and police components aside from what may be provided by their own governments prior to deployment. The UN has amassed valuable experience by now and is in a position to give training courses and to teach others to do so—regional organizations, in particular.

Training for Secretariat components could be institutionalized at Headquarters. Training could be provided by UN staff members for military and
civilian police components at training camps that several governments
have offered to make available; or, if no alternative is available, at the place
of deployment.

For deployment in situations of internal tension, a peace-keeping force,
in addition to having had specialized training, should include experts on
the country or region who—as circumstances permit—can work for conciliation between hostile groups and advise the force commander concerning
the conduct of the operation within the prevailing circumstances. The
United Nations follows the practice of designating a "lead" agency to
organize humanitarian assistance in conjunction with peace-keeping operations. For example, given the large numbers of refugees created by the
dissolution of the former Yugoslavia, the United Nations High Commissioner for Refugees was designated to lead the humanitarian effort in that
area, just as had been done almost twenty years earlier in Cyprus. This has
proved largely effective, notwithstanding some problems in communication and coordination. This practice can be perfected and expanded. Liaison
and coordination procedures at Headquarters and in the field between the
peace-keeping force and any functional agencies operating in the country
or region should be institutionalized so that all available resources can be
mobilized to meet the objectives of the operation.

Complex, potentially dangerous intrastate peace-keeping operations
such as the UN has undertaken in the former Yugoslavia, in Cambodia and
in Somalia demand disciplined, well-trained personnel equipped with
modern communications capability. One advantage that derives from the
end of the Cold War is that the former inhibitions against utilization of
troops from the five permanent members have fallen away. Russia, the
United Kingdom and France have all provided contingents for the peace-
keeping operation in Bosnia-Herzegovina and Croatia, China provided an
engineer battalion in Cambodia and the United States led the peace-enforcement operation in Somalia and is contributing forces to the preventive
peace-keeping operation in Macedonia. NATO and the WEU have together
developed procedures for ensuring through naval measures that the sanctions imposed by the Security Council against the former Yugoslavia are
not broken. The availability of troops from these sources, while it can
involve special problems, has substantially strengthened the capacity of the
United Nations to meet new peace-keeping demands.

As intrastate peacekeeping expands, account has to be taken of the
resistance of member states to any threat to national sovereignty that a
peace-keeping operation involved in essentially domestic matters might
entail. In this context, it would be helpful if the principle could be established, perhaps through a General Assembly debate on a report submitted
by the Secretary-General, that *peace-keeping action undertaken at the request of,*

or with the consent of, the government of the country of deployment cannot ipso facto, *violate the country's sovereignty.*

In discussing peacekeeping, the concentration has been on intrastate conflict situations, since that is the field in which there has been the greatest expansion of peacekeeping and it is also the most sensitive. It deserves to be reiterated here, however, as indicated in the previous chapter, that peacekeeping can also be used to deter conflict between states, as has been done successfully in Macedonia. There has been evidence in Cyprus and Southern Lebanon, however, that a lightly armed peace-keeping force cannot prevent a fully armed and determined force from invading. Therefore, any such deployment should be accompanied by a commitment of the Security Council to take appropriate measures under Chapter VII of the Charter if the peace-keeping force is attacked.

NOTES

1. General Assembly Resolution, 998 (ES-I), 4 November 1956.
2. Report of the Secretary-General, S/4382.
3. Security Council Resolution, 13, 1960.
4. The Congo became a member of the UN on September 20, 1960.
5. Report of the Secretary-General, S/4389.
6. Interview with Major General Indar Jit Rikhye, UN Oral History Collection, Yale University Library.
7. Security Council Resolution, 161, 1961.
8. OR, SC, 940th meeting, paragraphs 2–7; SG/1012, S/4727/add.2, Annex 4, February 20, 1961.
9. Brian Urquhart, *Hammarskjöld*, (New York: Harper and Row, 1972), p. 402.
10. Security Council Resolution, 186, 1964.
11. UN Document, S/5950.
12. UN Document, S/21982, 7 December 1990.
13. Security Council Resolution, 425, 1978.
14. UN Department of Public Information, *The Blue Helmets*, (New York, 1989). Also, Report of the Secretary-General, S/12611, 19 March 1978.
15. *Blue Helmets*, p. 385.
16. As part of the Central American Peace Process the UN is also involved in facilitating resolution of internal conflicts in El Salvador and (less directly) Guatemala.
17. Security Council Resolution, 644, 1989.
18. Letter dated 28 August 1989 from the UN Secretary-General to the President of the Security Council.
19. General Assembly Resolution, 43/24 (1988).
20. General Assembly Resolution, 45/2 (1990).
21. Security Council Resolution, 940 (31 July 1994).

4

Repelling Aggression and Enforcing Peace

MEETING AGGRESSION WITH MILITARY FORCE

There are two types of military enforcement action in which the United Nations can engage in the interest of peace. The first is action taken against an aggressor who has broken the peace or threatened to do so. This was seen at the time the UN was founded as the only justification for resort by the UN to military force. The UN Charter gives the Security Council the authority "to maintain or restore international peace and security," and to enforce the will of the Council on a state that has broken the peace. If peaceful means of dispute settlement as described in Chapter VI of the United Nations Charter fail, the Security Council may decide on sanctions to give effect to its decisions and if these also prove inadequate, it may take military action. Such use of force can best be identified as Article 42 enforcement measures since that article authorizes the Council to take "such action by air, sea or land forces as may be necessary to maintain or restore international peace and security."[1]

In such cases, the Council does not act as a neutral agent to bring an end to conflict between two warring parties; rather, as a party itself, the Council acts to defeat a country or countries whose guilt has been established by Council decision and protects the threatened party. Countries can thus in theory be protected from aggression by the United Nations through utilization of armed force.

According to Article 43 of the Charter, all UN members undertake "to make available to the Security Council on its call and in accordance with a special agreement or agreements, armed forces, assistance and facilities, including rights of passage, necessary for the purpose of maintaining international peace and security." There are no specified restrictions on the type or extent of force to be used for these purposes. In the first years of the United Nations the Military Staff Committee, at the direction of the Security Council, sought to reach agreement on how Article 43 should be implemented; it eventually produced a report on "General Principles Governing the Organization of Armed Forces Made Available to the Security Council by Member Nations."[2] However, primarily because of wide differences between the United States and the Soviet Union on the structure and mission of the forces to be made available to the Security Council, key issues remained unresolved. No agreements were ever reached and no troops for use by the Council, as foreseen in the passages quoted from the Charter, have been available. Therefore, in the only two instances in which Article 42-type action has been taken, the Security Council has called for, or authorized, the use of national forces to *enforce* the Council's resolutions.

KOREA

When North Korea attacked South Korea in 1950, the Council, in the temporary absence of the Soviet Union (which was boycotting the Council on the question of Chinese representation), adopted a resolution which identified the North Korean act as aggression and called on Member States to assist South Korea in resisting it. The Council recommended that "all Members providing military forces and other assistance pursuant to the . . . [relevant] Security Council resolutions make such forces and other assistance available to a unified command under the United States."[3] It requested further that the United States designate the commander of such forces and it authorized use of the UN flag by the unified command.

Thus, in the case of Korea the Security Council requested one member state to lead a combined effort on behalf of the United Nations to resist aggression by force. Notwithstanding his designation as commander of the unified forces in Korea, neither General Douglas MacArthur nor his successors ever sought or received instructions or guidance from the Security Council on the conduct of the war. Neither the Military Staff Committee that is mandated under the UN Charter to assist the Security Council in making plans "for the application of armed force" and to "advise and assist the Security Council on all questions relating to the Security Council's military requirements for the maintenance of peace and security," nor the Council itself, had any role in directing military operations in Korea.

The General Assembly, however, established a three-nation, cease-fire committee that sought a formula to end the war, and the Secretary-General suggested the procedure of direct talks between the military commanders, which was ultimately followed, and through which an armistice—but not peace—was achieved. But, as in the case of the military campaign, the commander of the unified forces in Korea carried out the protracted negotiations on the basis of instructions from Washington, not from the United Nations.

The advantages offered by the "Korean" procedure were

- An expeditious action to resist aggression. Only the United States had troops in East Asia that could be rapidly deployed for quick military action in Korea.
- The unambiguous command structure needed for large-scale field operations.
- A practical way to meet the responsibilities of the United Nations under the Charter in the absence of the multilateral force foreseen in Article 43.
- The validation of the concept of collective response to aggression. States acted jointly in response to Security Council (and subsequently General Assembly) decisions to defend a country under attack even though the country was not a UN member.

The disadvantages of this procedure (which became more evident in the course of time) were

- The lack of UN control or influence over the course of military action or over the precise purposes for which that action was taken (e.g., to repel and punish aggression or to reunify the peninsula under a freely elected government.)
- The identification of the military operation with the policy of the nation leading the effort rather than with the United Nations.
- The encouragement of division within the United Nations. Resistance grew to the dominant role of one member state pursuing goals not universally shared. Eventually a majority of member states disassociated themselves from the UN military role in Korea.
- The possibility for the aggressor to portray the collective action as the action of one country, the United States, rather than the response of the international community as a whole.

All of these disadvantages were intensified in the Korean case by the bitter disagreements that prevailed at the time between the United States and both the Soviet Union and the People's Republic of China. Under conditions of harmony among the permanent members of the Security Council, these various disadvantages can have considerably less force, as was the case in the Persian Gulf, but they will not be eliminated.

In the years between the Korean War and the Iraqi invasion of Kuwait, the United Nations did not respond militarily to threats to the peace or acts of aggression. Even on those rare occasions when the United States and the Soviet Union were in agreement during the Cold War, as in the Suez crisis in 1956, no UN army was fielded under Chapter VII of the UN Charter to *force* an invading army to withdraw. Peacekeeping was developed as a means of stabilizing a postconflict situation or, as described in the previous chapter, a preconflict situation in the Congo. It was characterized by Secretary-General Dag Hammarskjöld, who first deployed a true peace-keeping force, as a provisional measure under Article 40 of the Charter. According to this article the Security Council may call upon the parties concerned to comply with such provisional measures as it deems necessary or desirable, such provisional measures being "without prejudice to the rights, claims or position of the parties concerned." In peacekeeping the United Nations does not act as a party *against* another party as under Article 42, but rather, as a force between parties, without taking sides.

Only with the profound change in Soviet policy that led to an end of the Cold War did the necessary extent of agreement develop among the permanent members of the Security Council to permit resort to force in accordance with the principle of collective security.

KUWAIT

When Saddam Hussein initiated his action against Kuwait the permanent members were in general agreement that it must be resisted. To this degree the circumstances were radically different from those that prevailed at the time of the North Korean invasion of South Korea. In another sense they remained the same: No armed forces were available for the Security Council to deploy under the terms of Article 42 of the Charter. No agreements had been completed with member states on the provision of such troops.

Again, as in 1950, the Security Council relied on member states to use force, acting independently of UN command, to repel the aggression of a state that had been branded as aggressor by the Council. After imposing a comprehensive embargo in order to bring about Iraqi withdrawal and restoration of the legitimate government of Kuwait, the Council first called upon "those member states co-operating with the government of Kuwait which are deploying maritime forces to the area to use such measures commensurate to the specific circumstances as may be necessary under the authority of the Security Council . . . to ensure strict implementation" of the embargo.[4] Then, in resolution 678 of November 29, 1990, the Security Council authorized member states "to use all necessary means" to uphold and implement the earlier Council resolutions. All states were requested to provide appropriate support "for actions undertaken." This approach, taken with specific reference to Chapter VII of the Charter, constituted a modification of collective security as it had been implemented in Korea. As in the earlier enforcement action in Korea, the Council again turned to member states to act in its behalf through such measures as might be necessary. This time, however, no unified command was established and the use of the UN flag was not authorized.

The Gulf enforcement action was possible because the permanent members of the Security Council cooperated on a matter of peace and security in the way originally foreseen when the United Nations was founded. Representatives of the United States and the former Soviet Union repeatedly suggested at the time that such action was an important element in a new world order; that is, a world in which nations would be safe because of the capacity of the United Nations to guarantee their security through collective measures. This fundamental goal of the United Nations was unquestionably brought closer through the sustained cooperation and notably increased commonality of interests among the major powers. But serious questions remain as to a) whether the approach taken in the Gulf War constitutes a desirable model for enforcing the Council's decisions under Article 42 of the Charter; b) whether it could be successfully applied in other circumstances; and c) whether other options exist.

With regard to the first question, the action taken by the Council in response to the Iraqi aggression clearly constituted "effective collective measures for the prevention and removal of threats to the peace, and for the suppression of acts of aggression" as foreseen in Article 1 of the Charter. It authorized individual states to take "the necessary action" and requested all states "to provide appropriate support for the actions undertaken." Thus, all states were called on to assist in defending a state from aggression as specifically foreseen in Article 7 of the Charter. But the essential concept represented by Article 42 of the Charter is that troops and support will be available from member states for use *by the Security Council*—a truly United Nations force. The procedure of calling on individual states to take the necessary enforcement action without specified restrictions or limitations represents a necessary improvisation. It gave the Council, both in Korea and the Gulf, no means of controlling when, how or in what degree the enforcement measures were applied. States were only requested to keep the Council regularly informed.

Given the large extent of agreement that existed among the permanent members of the Security Council on the need to repel Iraqi aggression, and the very strong diplomatic and military leadership exercised by the United States, no serious dissent arose with regard to the actions taken against Iraq by the coalition forces. As the massively destructive campaign went forward under U.S. command, however, increasing unease became apparent among Council members and the wider UN membership on the proportionality of the means being used to achieve the objectives. President Bush and the coalition partners felt free to give their own interpretation to the Security Council resolutions. Had the United States decided to pursue the battle to Baghdad in order to eliminate Saddam Hussein, which might have been justified under a liberal interpretation of Resolution 678, serious differences would have developed within the Council and in the General Assembly. If support within the organization becomes fragmented, all the disadvantages that emerged from the Korean operation become operative. Moreover, if measures taken cease to have the endorsement of the majority of the Security Council, the question arises as to whether they can still be considered collective measures taken in the Council's behalf.

In assessing the future viability of the approaches followed in Korea and the Gulf, it must also be taken into account that they are not likely to be feasible unless the vital interests of one or more major military powers are at risk. (The military initiative taken by the United States in Somalia, when its vital interests were not endangered, will be considered later as a peace-enforcement action.) The United States has shown little interest in deploying substantial forces in Bosnia, for example, even though authorized to do so by the Security Council.

OTHER OPTIONS

With regard to the question of whether other options exist, there clearly are alternative procedures that might be followed by the Security Council that offer the prospect of effective Article 42 enforcement action without according unrestricted responsibility to individual member states or coalitions.

One option would be a variant of the procedure followed in Korea. National forces could be brought together in *ad hoc* fashion under a unified UN command, with the commander designated by whichever happened to be the major troop-contributing country. The problems that arose in Korea could be alleviated if the unified commander were required to consult with the Security Council, or with some form of military authority established by the Council, on the mission of the military operation and on the basic strategy to be followed in achieving it. The United States has resisted such a procedure in enforcement actions, most recently in Somalia, but its position may not be immutable given the fact that such a procedure would not give the Council an operational command function over the troops. It would have the distinct advantage of maintaining a close UN identification with all action taken and of giving the Security Council a decisive voice in defining strategic objectives. Moreover, it would lessen the possibility for one or more parties in a conflict to drive a wedge between the country commanding the force and other members of the United Nations.

Another theoretical option would be application of the procedure defined in Articles 42 and 43 of the Charter. For this to be feasible, the special agreements foreseen in Article 43 of the Charter, under which all members undertake "to make available to the Security Council on its call . . . armed forces, facilities and assistance," would have to be completed. Once such agreements were completed with a substantial number of member states that maintain effective military establishments, the Security Council would be able to call into being a multilateral force (land, sea and air) under a UN commander "to maintain or restore international peace and security." In such a military operation the commander appointed by the Security Council would have tactical authority but would operate under the guidance of the Security Council or a body established by the Council to serve this purpose. The Military Staff Committee, augmented by representatives of countries having a direct interest in the force, could, as foreseen when the Charter was drafted, "advise and assist the Security Council on all questions relating to military requirements." The committee would not hold command authority. This would be impractical since it functions on the basis of consensus. An enforcement operation using such troops would be clearly identified as a UN operation. Control would be firmly in the hands of the Security Council. The likelihood of sustained support for the action undertaken would be strong among UN members.

Taking account of the new opportunities that arose from the vast improvement in East/West relations, Secretary-General Boutros-Ghali recommended in *An Agenda for Peace* that the Security Council initiate negotiations on Article 43 agreements with willing states. In doing so, he recognized that the Security Council might never be able to organize an enforcement operation against a country having a major military capacity such as Iraq had when it invaded Kuwait. But in circumstances involving aggression or a threat to peace by a state of only modest military power, such a UN force could be effective and might well be the only kind of force available to deal with the situation.

The response among UN members to this particular suggestion of the Secretary-General was muted to say the least. Neither the General Assembly nor the Security Council, in their detailed and generally positive reviews of *An Agenda for Peace*, endorsed the proposal. In both organs the majority considered that it required "further study." The United States, in a presidential decision defining its policy on UN peace operations, expressed its opposition to entering into an Article 43 agreement with the UN.[5] Of the other permanent members of the Security Council only Russia has expressed interest in entering into such an agreement and other states have generally been unwilling to negotiate before the permanent members agree to do so. It is thus unlikely that even in the improved atmosphere of the post-Cold War era the multilateral earmarked fighting force foreseen in the Charter will be available to the Council.[6] This option can for practical purposes be ruled out.

A more realistic, but limited, option will be for the Security Council to call on regional organizations (rather than individual states) to undertake enforcement action as needed to meet threats to peace—something that would have been inconceivable during the Cold War. This is foreseen in Chapter VIII, Article 53 of the UN Charter. The Security Council successfully enlisted NATO air support to ensure the effective application of the sanctions imposed by the council against Yugoslavia, and subsequently to enforce a no-fly zone and provide air protection for UN peacekeepers and for designated protected locations in Bosnia.[7] The threat of air attacks caused the Bosnian Serbs to stop their bombardment of Sarajevo and Gorazde and NATO support proved effective elsewhere, even though command and control arrangements were awkward. The presidential policy decision on UN peace operations, already referred to, states that the United States will support peacekeeping by regional organizations provided it is endorsed by the UN Security Council and is conducted in accordance with Security Council criteria.[8]

Unfortunately, no regional organization comparable to NATO on which the UN can call for military support in enforcement operations exists in other geographic regions. Future possibilities in other areas are discussed in Chapter 7 on regional organizations.

PEACE ENFORCEMENT

As intrastate conflicts became prevalent in the late 1980s and the first years of the present decade, it became clear that in order to maintain peace the United Nations needed the possibility of taking enforcement action of a different nature—action to enforce peace and security between parties within countries rather than to defeat an external aggressor. In intrastate conflicts cease-fires were reached, sometimes repeatedly, only to be ignored by the parties. This was true in Croatia, Bosnia-Herzegovina, Somalia, Angola, Rwanda and in various of the new states in the former Soviet Union. In most of these cases the United Nations was requested to send peace-keeping forces to separate the parties, but the Secretary-General and member states generally felt this could not be done *until the cease-fire was demonstrably being honored*.[9] This has been the long-standing rule for peacekeeping. The result can be, and often was, continuation of the conflict. When the UN fails to take action in such cases as in Croatia for example, it appears impotent and incapable of fulfilling its first responsibility. Yet the reality has been that the UN has had no proper means of dealing with such situations.

To go into a country to stop the fighting between hostile elements who are intent on killing each other can be a dangerous undertaking. Third party intervention can only be successful if the military force deployed is equipped with adequate arms not only to respond to attacks against it, but also to isolate the parties from each other, to take artillery out of action, to impound weapons and to seal borders if arms are reaching one or both of the parties from external sources. This is far from the traditional peace-keeping mission and is not the kind of situation in which governments expect their troops to be placed if they are provided for peacekeeping—countries such as Canada that have been most forthcoming in supporting peace-keeping operations have expressed the fear that public support for peacekeeping will rapidly decline if their troops suffer serious casualties in a *peace-keeping* operation.

In situations where cease-fires are reached but not honored, to the extreme danger of the civilian population, something more than peacekeeping is needed. Yet it is not a situation in which an aggressor can be identified and military force applied under the terms of Article 42 of the Charter. What is required is a force provided by member states, to be deployed by authorization of the Security Council, not to fight against an aggressor but to force warring factions to comply with cease-fires to which they have agreed, and without taking the side of one or the other.

To meet this problem the concept of "peace-enforcement" was developed. Troops deployed for peace-enforcement are authorized to take forceful action in order to bring combatants to comply with the terms of a cease-fire, and they are adequately armed for this purpose. In *An Agenda for Peace*, Secretary-General Boutros-Ghali recommended that the Security Council "consider utilization of peace-enforcement units in clearly defined circumstances and with their terms of reference specified in advance." Boutros-Ghali stated that such peace-enforcement units would be available on call from member states "and would consist of troops that have volunteered for such service. They would have to be more heavily armed than peace-keeping forces and would need to undergo extensive preparatory training within their national forces."[10]

Peace-keeping and peace-enforcement missions as foreseen by the Secretary-General are distinctly different. Both fall within the category of provisional measures in terms of Article 40 of the Charter; neither is intended to resolve the basic problems underlying a conflict; for both, deployment is decided by the Security Council, troops are provided on a voluntary basis by member states and operations are carried out under the management of the Secretary-General. Peace-enforcement troops, however, are mandated to take offensive action as necessary to restore peace. Obviously, different kinds of training are required in the two cases (although they could be mutually compatible) and governments, in earmarking peace-enforcement units, would understand the more dangerous nature of their potential duty.

The reaction of member states was initially cautiously positive to Secretary Boutros-Ghali's recommendation on peace-enforcement units, but neither the Security Council nor the General Assembly officially endorsed the concept. It was nonetheless brought to reality by the force of events. The tragic events in Somalia and Bosnia allowed no escape from the logic of the Secretary-General's proposal. Developments there illustrated that conventional peace-keeping forces could not bring compliance with cease-fire agreements or afford adequate protection to ensure the safety of humanitarian operations under conditions of armed conflict or anarchy. Peace-enforcement units, as defined in *An Agenda for Peace*, were needed. In the desperate situation of violence and conflict in Somalia the Security Council approved actions on an *ad hoc* basis that amounted to realization of the peace-enforcement concept. Unfortunately, the need for peace-enforcement, and the possibility of agreement on its application, came before the UN or its members were adequately prepared.

YUGOSLAVIA

The inadequacy of traditional peacekeeping to halt a tragic conflict became evident when, with the breakup of the former Yugoslavia, fighting erupted between the Croats and Serbs in newly independent Croatia. Given the high state of tension that existed throughout the former Yugoslavia, there was no doubt that the situation in Croatia (and briefly in Slovenia) constituted a threat to international security. UN action to restore peace was clearly called for. Action was delayed, however, and when it came it was inadequate.

No effort will be made here to recount in detail the complex course of events in which the UN was involved in the bitter ethnic strife that occurred in the former Yugoslavia. Instead, only the progression of developments will be sketched that were directly relevant to the adequacy, or inadequacy, of the UN's efforts to bring an end to the fighting.

It is necessary to begin in Croatia where Croat and Serbian forces, after intense fighting, reached repeated agreements on cease-fires and requested the United Nations to send a peace-keeping force. The request was rejected on the ground that a peace-keeping force can only be deployed after a cease-fire is operative and the fighting has stopped. The fighting continued with increasing destruction and loss of life. Only after a cease-fire that held was reached, through the mediation of a special UN envoy, was a large peace-keeping force sent to monitor its provisions. The force was, as is traditional, equipped with light arms that it was authorized to use only in self-defense. While UNPROFOR was largely successful in preventing a recurrence of the fighting in Croatia, it was unable to overcome resistance of the parties to implementation of important provisions of the cease-fire, such as the sequestering of all heavy weapons and the return of refugees.

UNPROFOR Headquarters was established in Sarajevo. While it had no mandate with regard to Bosnia, the hope was that by its presence it would discourage the outbreak there of hostilities. Unfortunately, its presence did not have this effect. After civil war erupted in Bosnia-Herzegovina UNPRO-FOR headquarters was removed, leaving only 100 military and civilian staff in Sarajevo to promote local cease-fires (which were repeatedly achieved, only to be ignored) and humanitarian activities. Subsequently, the UNPRO-FOR staff in Sarajevo was enlarged to secure the airport and to supervise the withdrawal of antiaircraft weapons and the collection of heavy weapons at agreed locations in the city.

UNPROFOR was initially mandated for action in Bosnia, as in Croatia, as a traditional peace-keeping force. It was authorized, as is normal in peace-keeping operations, to take such action as necessary against any attempt to prevent by force the carrying out of its mission. The mandate was subsequently strengthened to authorize the use of "all necessary means" to ensure delivery of humanitarian assistance. However, the peace-keeping troops were too limited in number and inadequately armed to attempt to break through the indigenous forces that often blocked the transport routes and hampered relief operations. The UN troops remained peace-keeping forces. As such they could alleviate a desperate situation but they could not provide the security needed for the uninterrupted delivery of relief assistance or to bring compliance with the repeated cease-fires that were reached in Sarajevo and elsewhere in the country.

While relying on peace-keeping troops on the ground, the Security Council, acting under Chapter VII of the Charter, imposed an embargo on arms shipments to all states of the former Yugoslavia[11] and comprehensive economic sanctions against Serbia and Montenegro. The situation in Bosnia nonetheless went from bad to worse.

Despite repeated Security Council resolutions demanding the cessation of Bosnian Serb attacks, the Serb bombardment of Sarajevo was intensified and isolated Bosnian Muslim centers were kept under siege. In the face of an increasingly desperate situation the United Nations moved cautiously toward peace-enforcement measures. The Security Council first called on states to take nationally, or through regional agencies, "all measures neces-sary" to facilitate the delivery of humanitarian assistance to Sarajevo and wherever needed in other parts of Bosnia.[12] This was an invitation to NATO to use air force against the attacking Bosnian Serbs. Countries having peace-keeping soldiers on the ground were fearful that they would be harmed as a result of such action, however, so none took place.

After repeated Security Council resolutions demanding the cessation of Bosnian Serb attacks were ignored, the Council established a "no-fly" zone over Bosnia[13] to be enforced by NATO. The Council declared Sarajevo and the other besieged towns "safe areas, free from armed attacks and from any other hostile acts which endanger the well-being and the safety of their inhabitants."[14] The deployment of additional military observers was authorized to monitor the humanitarian situation in the safe areas. A month later, the Council decided that member states, acting nationally or through regional organizations, might take "all necessary measures, through the use of air power, in and around the safe areas . . . to support UNPROFOR in the performance of its mandate."[15] At the same time, the Council expanded the UNPROFOR mandate to authorize it to "take the necessary measures, including the use of force, in reply to bombardments against the safe areas by any of the parties or to armed incursion into them or in the event of any deliberate obstruction in or around those areas to the freedom of movement of UNPROFOR or of protected humanitarian convoys."

The Council took this action with direct reference to Chapter VII of the Charter. The peace-keeping operation was thus altered in midstream to a form of peace-enforcement. But the troops remained too few and inadequately armed to counter the Serb attacks on Sarajevo or even to reach the other protected towns. Finally, when the situation in Sarajevo, as shown on television around the world, became intolerable, the United Nations gave an ultimatum to the Serbs to cease the bombardment of the city and withdraw their heavy weapons to a distance of twelve miles from the city or face air attacks by NATO. (NATO had already agreed that it would take such action on request of the Secretary-General.) This enforcement threat had the desired effect as it did subsequently in Gorazde, another besieged Bosnian "safe area."

Thus, peace-enforcement action was taken in Bosnia with hesitation and without the presence of UN forces deployed to the country for this purpose. The troops were provided by contributing countries for peace-keeping action. The contributors were therefore understandably reluctant to see their contingents placed in the increased danger that enforcement involved. The result was a lack of clarity of purpose and a hesitancy in taking action that seriously jeopardized the credibility of the United Nations and permitted the conflict to take an unnecessary toll. Beginning in Croatia, the traditional concept of peacekeeping was inadequate to lend the UN the credibility it needed to bring early and full compliance with a cease-fire in Croatia or to prevent the war from spreading, with terrible consequences, to Bosnia.

SOMALIA

Partly as a result of the experience in Croatia, the need for peace-enforcement action was recognized at any earlier stage in the crisis in Somalia. Peace-enforcement, as foreseen in *An Agenda for Peace*, was unambiguously authorized by the Security Council—for the first time in the UN's history—and knowingly undertaken by contributing states at the time of deployment, although there were no volunteer units available.

In March 1992 the United Nations, in association with the Organization of African Unity, the Arab League and the Islamic Conference, succeeded in negotiating a cease-fire agreement between the principal warring factions in Mogadishu. The agreement provided for fifty unarmed UN military observers to monitor the cease-fire in Mogadishu and a UN security component for convoys of humanitarian assistance travelling to other points in the country. The security, or peace-keeping, force was to provide UN relief convoys with a sufficiently strong military escort to deter attack; but they were authorized to fire only in self-defense "as a last resort if deterrence should not prove effective."[16]

The factions did not comply with the cease-fire's provisions and the unarmed monitors had no means of forcing them to do so. A modest peace-keeping or "security" force, consisting of 500 Pakistani troops, was deployed to afford security for relief efforts in the capital. The force was largely immobilized by the violence and looting that dominated the city. In light of the deteriorating situation throughout the country, the Security Council approved the deployment of four additional UN security units, each with a strength of up to 750, to be stationed in four operational zones of the country. In each there would be a consolidated UN effort to carry out relief and recovery programs, to monitor the cease-fire and contain potential hostilities, to oversee security, demobilization and disarmament and encourage a peace process through conciliation, mediation and good offices.

All in all the Security Council authorized the deployment of 4,219 peace-keeping troops to bring security in the conditions of anarchy and violence that engulfed the entire country. However, having only a peace-keeping mandate, they could not be deployed outside Mogadishu, since various de facto Somali authorities refused to concur and conditions were such as to make the dispatch of lightly armed soldiers unacceptably dangerous. The major humanitarian effort that nongovernmental organizations and UN agencies were seeking to carry out came to a practical halt. Under these circumstances action was taken that set not only an important precedent but provided a new definition of international security in the post–Cold War world.

The United States Government, spurred by the vivid media portrayal of the horrors of famine and violence in Somalia, informed Secretary-General Boutros-Ghali on November 25, 1992, that "if the Security Council were to decide to authorize Member States to use forceful means to ensure the delivery of relief supplies to the people of Somalia, the United States would be ready to take the lead in organizing and commanding such an operation."[17] The United States was prepared to provide as many as 32,000 troops for the enterprise. Just the day before, the Secretary-General had addressed a letter to the Security Council President in which he described the gravity of the situation in Somalia. He ended by saying that "the conditions that have developed in Somalia . . . make it exceedingly difficult for the United Nations operation to achieve the objectives approved by the Security Council. I am giving urgent consideration to this state of affairs and do not exclude the possibility that it may become necessary to review the basic premises and principles of the United Nations effort in Somalia."[18] This is precisely what the American action forced him and the Security Council to do. The question was posed: What can the United Nations legitimately undertake to stop an intrastate conflict or major humanitarian catastrophe when traditional peacekeeping is inadequate?

The Secretary-General put this question to the Security Council in the form of five options.

1. To continue efforts to deploy a larger peace-keeping force (UNOSOM) that would operate according to the existing principles and practices of United Nations peace-keeping operations. He did not feel this would be an adequate response to the humanitarian crisis in Somalia.

2. To abandon the idea of using international military personnel to protect humanitarian activities, withdraw the existing peace-keeping force and leave the humanitarian agencies to negotiate the best arrangements they could with the various faction and clan leaders. He excluded this "withdrawal" option with the conclusion that the current difficulties were due not to the presence of the peacekeepers but to the fact that not enough of them were there and they did not have the right mandate.

3. To undertake a show of force with UNOSOM in Mogadishu in the expectation that this might create conditions there for the safe delivery of humanitarian relief and deter the various armed groups there and elsewhere in Somalia from withholding cooperation from UNOSOM.

4. To carry out a country-wide *enforcement* operation undertaken by a group of member states authorized to do so by the Security Council.

5. To undertake a country-wide *enforcement* operation under United Nations command and control. He noted that the Secretariat did not have the capability to command and control an operation of the

size and urgency required by the crisis. Member states contributing troops for the operation would therefore have to provide not only troops but also personnel for the command and control headquarters in the field and in New York. Moreover, they would have to accept that the staff officers would take orders from the United Nations and not from their national authorities.

Boutros-Ghali emphasized that there was no alternative but to resort to Chapter VII of the Charter, that is *enforcement*. He preferred that if forceful action were taken, it be under UN command and control. If the fourth option were chosen instead, he suggested various means of linking the operation to the United Nations. The countries undertaking the action could be asked to furnish the Security Council with regular reports, for example, on the basis of which the Council could, at specified intervals, review the authority it had given for the operation to take place. The Council might also clearly establish the purpose of the operation and provide that as soon as the purpose was accomplished, the operation would be replaced by a UN peace-keeping operation. The Secretary-General obviously had some of the unsatisfactory aspects of the conduct of the Gulf War in mind.

The Security Council unanimously voted in favor of option four, welcoming the United States offer and authorizing the member states "cooperating in implementation of the offer . . . *to use all necessary means* [i.e., force] to establish as soon as possible a secure environment for humanitarian relief operations in Somalia." In a notably vague paragraph the Council authorized the "Secretary-General and the member states concerned to make the necessary arrangements for the unified command and control of the forces involved which will reflect the offer referred to above [the American offer]."[19]

The United States informally proposed to carry out the action under the UN flag but Boutros-Ghali opposed this on the ground that the UN would not actually be in control.

The Somalia resolution contained the following preambular paragraph that is of major significance:

Determining that the magnitude of the human tragedy caused by the conflict in Somalia, further exacerbated by the obstacles being created for the quick distribution of humanitarian assistance, *constitutes a threat to international peace and security* [Emphasis added].

This was the first time that an internal humanitarian crisis had been defined as a threat to international peace and security justifying the use of enforcement measures under Chapter VII of the Charter. The use of all appropriate force was authorized to *enforce* compliance with a cease-fire agreement and put an end to violence as necessary to permit the safe delivery of humanitarian assistance.

The mission of the American-led operation, UNITAF, was limited to establishing a secure environment for humanitarian relief operations in Somalia, despite the strongly expressed views of Secretary-General Boutros-Ghali that it should also be responsible for disarming the various armed factions. The mission, having the advantage of the most modern arms and well-trained soldiers, was successfully accomplished with few casualties. Free movement for relief shipments was restored except for the northern, self-declared, independent portion of Somalia that had not been included in the UNITAF operation. Starvation was eliminated. In a complementary effort to establish a basis for peace, the Secretary-General convened a preparatory meeting in Addis Ababa for a national reconciliation conference in which a total of fourteen Somali political movements took part. Agreement was reached on implementing the cease-fire and on modalities of disarmament. Subsequently, the national reconciliation conference opened, also in Addis Ababa, on March 15, 1993, and on March 27 the Addis Ababa Agreements were signed that constituted the basis for the resolution of the political problems of Somalia. It appeared that the worst of the Somalia crisis might be over, although the extensive arms still in the hands of the various factions was an evident cause for concern.

In his proposals to the Security Council for the UN force to replace UNITAF, Boutros-Ghali recommended that the tasks of the replacement UN Force, UNOSOM II, should include the following:

- To monitor compliance with the cessation of hostilities and all other agreements to which the parties have agreed.
- To take appropriate action against any faction that violates or threatens to violate the cessation of hostilities.
- To maintain control of the heavy weapons of the organized factions pending their destruction or transfer to a newly constituted national army.
- To seize the small arms of all unauthorized armed elements and assist in the registration and security of such arms.
- To maintain the security of all ports, airports and lines of communications required for the delivery of humanitarian assistance.
- To protect the personnel, installations and equipment of the UN and non-governmental humanitarian organizations *and take such forceful action as may be required to neutralize armed elements that attack, or threaten to attack, such facilities and personnel, pending the establishment of a new Somali police force which can assume this responsibility* (Emphasis added).

- To continue the program for mine-clearing.
- To assist in the repatriation of refugees and displaced persons within Somalia.

This was a far broader and more difficult mandate than UNITAF had been given. In his report to the Council, Boutros-Ghali stated that the threat to international security that the Security Council had earlier found to exist still persisted. Consequently, in order to carry out these objectives UNOSOM II would have to be "endowed with enforcement powers under Chapter VII of the Charter."[20] The highest priority of UNOSOM II, however, was defined as support for the efforts of the Somali people "in promoting the process of national reconciliation and the establishment of democratic institutions."[21] The mission combined the military task of peace enforcement with the political task of peace-building. UNOSOM II was intended to establish, in conjunction with the Addis Ababa Agreements, a basis for the restoration of stable government in Somalia.

Thus the United Nations undertook for the first time a major *peace-enforcement* operation under the control of the Secretary-General, a concept that the Security Council had not (and still has not) approved in principle, and one that the Secretary-General said at the time of the initial American-led Somali operation the United Nations was not equipped in terms of command and control to carry out. This proved to be accurate, with extremely unfortunate consequences.

No detailed, impartial account is yet publicly available of the operational problems of UNOSOM II, although the contents of one prepared for the Security Council by an international commission have become widely known. Enough is clear about this first UN-led peace-enforcement undertaking to permit a number of conclusions to be drawn that are important as the UN is involved more and more in the resolution of internal armed crises.

IMPARTIALITY

An essential requirement in peace-enforcement, just as in peacekeeping, is strict impartiality. As a provisional measure, peace-enforcement must be without prejudice to the rights, claims or positions of the parties concerned. In Mogadishu, however, where the competing political leaders were resident with their separate militias, political impartiality was not—perhaps could not be—maintained. UNOSOM II took sides and, in seeking to determine the future political leadership in Somalia, became a party to the conflict.

General Mohamed Farah Aideed, the leader of a political faction known as SNA, had long had a prominent role in Somali politics. He had taken the lead in unseating the Somali dictator Said Barre. He was well-known to Secretary-General Boutros-Ghali as a disruptive element in Egyptian-led attempts to resolve the political crisis that followed the fall of Said Barre. Aideed had signed the cease-fire agreement along with his arch-rival but he did not cooperate with the UN observer and peace-keeping missions provided for in the agreement. In a report to the Security Council on November 27, 1992, the Secretary-General identified General Aideed by name as responsible for a number of disturbing actions aimed at UNOSOM I.[22] There was good reason, then, for the leaders of UNOSOM II to view Aideed with special concern. There was also a reasonable basis for Aideed to believe that the UN was hostile toward him. He is said to have known that the United Nations was secretly planning to capture his Mogadishu radio station. The U.S. Liaison Mission in Mogadishu, which was closely involved in the UN operation, appears inadvertently to have signaled to Aideed an intention to marginalize him and his clan.[23] The preference of the leadership of UNOSOM II, which was largely American, was evident.

On June 4, 1993, UNOSOM officers informed Mohammed Hassan Awale Qaibdid, a close associate of General Aideed, that a designated weapons storage site in the same building as Aideed's radio station would be inspected on the following day. Qaibdid responded that the inspection must not take place; if it did, it would lead to "war." UNOSOM nonetheless proceeded with its plan. On the next morning UN soldiers, in trying to control a demonstration in front of Radio Mogadishu, shot and killed a Somali. Shortly thereafter, Pakistani forces were sent on the inspection mission in southern Mogadishu in unarmored vehicles, despite the warning from General Aideed's associate. Coming under coordinated attack, twenty-four were killed and over one hundred wounded, many seriously.

General Aideed claimed that the attacks on the UN troops were a spontaneous response to the killing of the Somali earlier in the day. The leaders of UNOSOM II concluded that the attack had been planned and executed by General Aideed and his forces as an immediate response to the UN effort to inspect the weapons storage site, but with the broader intent of crippling the UNOSOM II mission. An independent expert, Professor Tom Farer of American University, who was engaged by the UN Special Representative in Somalia, Admiral Howe, to carry out an investigation, agreed. He found the UNOSOM conclusion valid and indisputable.[24]

The United Nations responded to the attack on the Pakistanis as a criminal act for which General Aideed was responsible. The UN decided to seek his arrest[25] and offered a monetary reward for assistance in finding the general. Once Aideed was categorized as an enemy, the UN action ceased to have the character of a provisional measure. A futile search for Aideed led to serious confrontations between the American peacekeepers and Somalis in which many Somalis were killed. The culmination was on October 3, when U.S. Rangers, on yet another mission to capture Aideed, were caught in a firefight with Somali militia. Seventeen Americans were killed and many more wounded. The number of Somalis killed is still not known.

The death of the Americans caused a strong outcry in the American Congress and wide criticism in the media. Responding to these developments, President Clinton gave orders to the American forces in Somalia—without consulting the United Nations—to stop hunting Aideed. Subsequently, he announced that all U.S. forces would be withdrawn by the end of March, 1994. The Security Council decided, in turn, that emphasis should again be placed on a political solution to the Somali problem, implying that military enforcement measures would not be pursued. The effort to achieve disarmament by force was abandoned.[26] General Aideed emerged from hiding and was flown in an American plane to participate on equal terms in a further conference on national unity in Addis Ababa. There was no longer a designated enemy. But the unhappy developments that led to this return to impartiality had raised serious questions as to the viability of the concept of peace enforcement.

(FAMILIARITY WITH CULTURE AND POLITICS)

Peace-enforcement and the successful building of peace in disintegrated societies requires careful planning based on a full understanding of the culture and politics of the country or countries involved. This was not entirely absent in the Somalia operation as evidenced by the considerable success achieved in restoring social stability in areas outside of Mogadishu.[27] At the political center, however, in Mogadishu, the inadequacy of the UN's preparation brought near disaster. The power and influence of the clan leaders was not adequately assessed nor was their individual importance in bringing about national reconciliation. The likely reaction of a man like Aideed to actions that threatened the position of his clan was not sufficiently appreciated; neither was the reaction of the Somali population appreciated when a Somali leader was attacked by an outside force, which the United Nations remained.

COMMAND AND CONTROL

There were clearly grave command and control failures in the UNOSOM II operation. At times there appears to have been no effective unified command at all. Various national contingents responded to orders from their national chain of command. The Italian contingent refused to follow the directives of the Force Commander. The authority of the Secretary-General in the overall direction of the operation lacked credibility. Eventually, the Americans appeared to dominate the operation, acting largely independently of UN control (although a frequent criticism in the United States was that the American forces were being endangered by serving under non-American command).

TRAINING

Peace-enforcement requires special training. An obvious weakness of the Somalia military operation was the failure of the various national contingents to work effectively together. This was partly a command problem. But it also derived from the absence of common training on how to deal with volatile domestic situations. Neither the military nor the civilian leadership was adequately prepared for the problems inherent in enforcing peace in the absence of cooperation from one or more of the parties concerned. A recent study shows that, in regular peace-keeping operations, the number of casualties in units that have had special training for peace-keeping service is far lower than in those that have not.[28] No similar study has been made of a peace-enforcement action but it is likely that the positive effect of training would be shown to be even greater.

WHITHER PEACE ENFORCEMENT?

There has been widespread criticism of the utilization of military force by the UN both in the former Yugoslavia and in Somalia. From the foregoing accounts, it is evident that serious mistakes were made in both cases. It is instructive to note, however, that the criticism of the two operations is, in very general terms, based on opposite grounds. In the case of Yugoslavia, the charge (in which the author concurs) is that the enforcement measures taken were too little and too late. In the case of Somalia, the charge is that enforcement efforts were precipitate and impractical, an assessment that this observer considers shortsighted.

It appears beyond question that the traditional peace-keeping mandate was inadequate to bring an end to the fighting in Yugoslavia. The credible threat of the application of strong military force was necessary in order to stop the Serb attacks. The transition from an operation conceived as peacekeeping to an enforcement action complicated the operation, suggesting the need for careful assessment and planning before an operation is initiated in an intrastate conflict.

In Somalia the initial peace-enforcement action, UNITAF, was highly successful, achieving quick results that a peace-keeping operation almost certainly could not have done. Peacekeeping had been demonstrably incapable of maintaining the cease-fire in Mogadishu. For this purpose enforcement measures were also needed.

From these two experiences the conclusion that emerges is that peace-enforcement is a much needed addition to the tools available to the United Nations in seeking to end internal conflict. It also emerges that the United Nations and member states have much to learn, and many adjustments to make, in applying the concept in the future. Some progress has already been made. A state-of-the-art operations center has been established at UN Headquarters through which constant communication with field operations is now possible. The importance of pursuing a political track simultaneously with peace-enforcement measures is now better understood, as is the need for fuller background information on the historical, social and political circumstances in deciding whether peacekeeping or peace-enforcement is the right course to follow.

Command and control will remain a complex problem in multilateral enforcement actions. In the light of the Somali and Yugoslav experiences, it appears desirable to remove the Secretary-General from operational responsibility when enforcement measures are to be taken. To be of assistance in the ultimate resolution of the conflict—that is, in peacemaking—the Secretary-General needs to remain above the fray. His impartiality will be in jeopardy if he is the one ultimately responsible for the decision to bomb one party or another. This is a task better assumed by the Security Council or an organization acting in its behalf.

To ensure greater success for future enforcement actions one responsibility lies mainly with governments. It will be extremely important that member states comply with the Secretary-General's recommendation that they earmark and train specified troop units (preferably of volunteers) for enforcement-type duties. It will also be important for countries with extensive military resources, especially those like the United States that have indicated they do not intend to earmark specific units for UN duty, to keep in readiness the equipment that would be needed for peace-enforcement actions. It would be a useful function of the long-idle Military Staff Committee to draw up an inventory of materiel for which a need can be foreseen and work out with member states what each can best supply.

NOTES

1. Security Council Resolution S/1511, 27 June 1950.
2. SCOR 2d Year, Special supplement No. 1, S/336, 30 April 1947.
3. Security Council Resolution S/1588, 7 July 1950.
4. Security Council Resolution 665, 25 August 1990.
5. Presidential Decision Directive 25, 3 May 1994.

6. In 1992, the Foreign Relations Committee of the U.S. Senate expressed strong support for the negotiation of an Article 43 agreement between the United States and the United Nations. This was not endorsed, however, by the full Senate.

7. See Security Council Resolutions 824 (1993), 836 (1993), 844 (1993), and 908 (1994).

8. The NATO treaty refers to Article 51 (the right of self-defense) but makes no mention of Article 53. When the U.S. Senate was considering ratification of the NATO Treaty, Secretary of State Dean Acheson testified that NATO would not be subject to orders of the Security Council. This appears to be the accepted principle and the availability of NATO forces will always be dependent on the agreement of the NATO Council. In the Croatian and Bosnian cases, the relevant Security Council resolutions refer to the participation of regional organizations in enforcement action as voluntary.

9. This principle is specifically endorsed in the U.S. Presidential Policy Declaration of May 3, 1994.

10. The earmarking and training of troops and the stockpiling of equipment for such a purpose is not an entirely new idea. During the Korean War the General Assembly recommended that each member state maintain within its armed forces earmarked units so trained that they could promptly be made available for service "as a United Nations unit or units." This was before the peace-keeping concept was developed. Presumably, therefore, these troops were foreseen for enforcement purposes, although it was not specifically so stated. In any event, member states did not comply with the recommendation. Subsequent recommendations by Secretaries-General and various external organizations were for the earmarking and training only of *peace-keeping* forces.

11. Security Council Resolution 713, 1992.

12. Security Council Resolution 770, 1992.

13. Security Council Resolution 781, 1992.

14. Security Council Resolution S/RES/824, 1993.

15. Security Council Resolution S/RES/836, 1993.

16. See Security Council Resolution 751, 1992, establishing the United Nations Operation in Somalia (UNOSOM).

17. UN Document S/24868, 30 November 1992.

18. Security Council Resolution 751, 1992.

19. Security Council Resolution 794, 3 December 1992.

20. Security Council Document S/25354, 3 March 1993.

21. Security Council Resolution S/RES/886, 1993.

22. UN Document S/24859, 27 November 1992.

23. See the article "From Warlord to Peacelord" in the *Washington Post*, September 12, 1993, by Tom Farer. Farer was engaged by the Secretary-

General to carry out an independent investigation of the June 5, 1993, attack on UN peacekeepers.

24. UN Document S/26351, 24 August 1993.

25. Security Council Resolution 837, 6 June 1993.

26. Security Council Resolution 897, 1994.

27. Report of the Secretary-General to the Security Council S/1994/12, 6 January 1994.

28. Barry M. Blechman and J. Matthew Vaccaro, "Training for Peacekeeping, The United Nations' Role." A report of the Henry L. Stimson Center, April 6, 1994.

5

Building Peace

Preventive diplomacy is generally seen—as it has been in Chapter 2—as action to be taken in response to a critical situation that threatens to lead to conflict. The prevention of conflict, however, has a larger dimension. Over the long term, the surest way to prevent conflict is to eliminate its root causes. Conditions of life must be achieved that will permit peoples to live in harmony with each other under democratic governance that in itself will serve as a deterrent to war.[1] The term "peace-building" has come into use to describe what needs to be done to bring about these conditions, or, at least, to make progress toward this goal. Peace-building can be seen as the macro approach to the prevention of war. It can too easily be dismissed as overly idealistic and vague, as beyond the human capacity and certainly beyond that of existing multilateral organizations.

The danger of conflict is apparent, often intrastate in nature, that results from social and economic causes and of humanitarian disasters that in their consequences can be equated with war. With the end of the Cold War more resources and greater attention should, in principle, be available to alleviate these problems than has been the case since the United Nations was founded. It can be argued that the disappearance of the rivalry between the United States and the USSR will result in *less* rather than more attention being paid to the needs of the poorer countries since they are no longer competing for strategic advantage in Third World countries, and, further, that any resources released from Cold War related objectives will be directed toward relief of the budgetary problems of the rich countries rather than the development needs of the poorest. All of this is doubtless true. Beyond that, the successor states to the USSR are not economically able to provide aid to developing countries, a category into which many of them now fall.

But it is also evident that governments are beginning to accept a measure of responsibility for human well-being and are coming to realize—if only slowly—that investment in removing the underlying causes of conflict, whether interstate or intrastate, is an investment in their own security. Western countries, for example, have been willing to make large financial outlays in the interest of social and political stability in Russia. The United States invested a substantial amount of money in UNITAC to alleviate a social crisis in Somalia, notwithstanding its own budgetary problems (and its indebtedness to the UN). Still, it will take strong intellectual and political leadership to bring about a wide public understanding of the commonality of interest in deterring conflict through peace-building measures, that should now bind the countries of the world together.

The United Nations can fill an important leadership role by establishing as the goal of a new era of fundamentally changed international relations the construction of a foundation for lasting peace. This may not sound very different from long-articulated UN ideals. What is new is the opportunity to pursue this objective in a greatly changed environment and with a revised assessment of what is—or should be—possible. The United Nations system should take the lead in developing, in cooperation with member states, the concepts, programs and new instrumentalities needed for progress toward this goal and in defining the complexities, difficulties and likely setbacks that will be entailed.

POSTCONFLICT PEACE-BUILDING

In *An Agenda for Peace* Secretary-General Boutros-Ghali addressed only postconflict peace-building, defining it as "action to identify and support structures which will tend to strengthen and solidify peace in order to avoid a relapse into conflict." He suggested that it might include disarming the previously warring parties and the restoration of order, repatriation of refugees, advisory and training support for security personnel, monitoring elections, advancing efforts to protect human rights, reforming or strengthening governmental institutions and promoting formal and informal processes of political participation. These are realistic objectives that have since the end of the Cold War been successfully realized in various instances. Notable examples are the preparation and monitoring of elections in Nicaragua, the repatriation of some 300,000 refugees in Cambodia, and the contribution to institution building in Namibia.

There are also examples of failure: in Haiti, where effectively monitored elections did not lead to stable democratic governments, and Angola, where the collection of weapons was imperfect and free elections did not prevent the resumption of civil war. It should not be expected that such undertakings will always succeed in establishing a basis of sustainable peace. A concept that entails such a high degree of idealism needs to be leavened with a healthy appreciation of reality if disillusionment is to be avoided. As one assesses the value of peace-building, analysis of the causes of failures will be as important as analysis of success. The world media can be counted on for assistance in this regard. At the same time, failures should not be allowed to overshadow successes or invalidate the concept of peace-building.

PEACE-BUILDING IN ITS BROADER DIMENSION

When seen in a larger context than postconflict situations, peace-building assumes even broader dimensions. It encompasses all actions and programs that can contribute to the deterrence of conflict and the strengthening of international security. This statement immediately raises the question: what is meant today by international security? As has been noted earlier, when the United Nations Charter was signed, international security meant that countries would not be subject to external attack or the threat of attack. Now, with the increased interdependence of peoples as well as of states, and the transparency that brings instantaneous global awareness of all serious threats to human well-being, the common understanding of international security has changed and continues to evolve.

In his 1991 Annual Report to the General Assembly, Secretary-General Pérez de Cuéllar wrote, "I believe that the protection of human rights has now become one of the keystones of the arch of peace." And further, "The case for not impinging on the sovereignty, territorial integrity and political independence of States is indubitably strong. But it would only be weakened if it were to carry the implication that sovereignty, even in this day and age, includes the right of mass slaughter or the launching of systematic campaigns of decimation or forced exodus of civilian populations in the name of controlling civil strife or insurrection."[2] In Somalia the Security Council determined that a grave humanitarian crisis was a threat to international security. Thus international security has come to mean the security of peoples within states from natural disaster, from civil conflict, or from massive violation of human rights as well as the security of one state from attack by another.

DEFINING INTERNATIONAL SECURITY

To maintain international security can now be reasonably interpreted as connoting the protection of states and peoples from mortal harm. Therefore, to build peace must include action to both promote friendly relations between states and to encourage a harmonious social environment within states. This concept is, indeed, wide reaching, and, if accepted, indicates the broad dimensions of peace-building. Peace-building needs to be seen as having many components—blocks in an edifice that, like the great cathedrals, will take generations to build. Secretary-General Boutros-Ghali has suggested that peace-building should be viewed as the counterpart of preventive diplomacy, which seeks to avoid the breakdown of peaceful conditions. But peace-building must also be seen as *preventive diplomacy* in its largest form. It is intended both to remove the underlying causes of conflict and to prevent its recurrence should conflict break out.

Peace-building measures can be undertaken to overcome political, economic or social weaknesses in national, regional and global societies. Such measures are foreseen in the first article of the UN Charter, in which a principal purpose of the United Nations is defined as achieving "international co-operation in solving international problems of an economic, social, cultural or humanitarian character, and in promoting respect for human rights and fundamental freedoms for all." At the end of the founding conference in San Francisco, the American Secretary of State, sounding much like the UN Secretary-General today, had the following to say:

> In the next twenty-five years the development of the economic and social foundations of peace will be of paramount importance. If the United Nations cooperate effectively toward an expanding world economy, better living conditions for all men and women, and closer understanding among peoples, they will have gone far toward eliminating in advance the causes of another world war. . . . If they fail, there will be instead widespread depressions and economic warfare which would fatally undermine the world organization. *No provisions that can be written into the Charter will enable the Security Council to make the world secure from war if men and women have no security in their homes and in their jobs*[3] (Emphasis added).

It can be said, then, that the United Nations system, encompassing its functional offices and specialized agencies, has been engaged in peace-building from the time of its establishment.

Inis Claude, in his insightful book *Swords into Plowshares*, refers to "the functional approach to peace," stating that functional activities "which flourish luxuriantly in the United Nations" are immediately and explicitly concerned with such values as prosperity, welfare, social justice, and the "good life." Functionalism, he states, "envisages its task in terms of the alteration of the subjective conditions of mankind. War is caused by the attitudes, habits of thought and feeling, that are fostered by the state system. Functional organizations may, by focusing attention upon areas of common interest, build habits of cooperation which will equip human beings for the conduct of a system of international relations in which the expectation of constructive collaboration will replace that of sterile conflict as the dominant motif."[4] Claude thus interprets social progress as a way of encouraging cooperation between states that will contribute to peace between states. This was clearly in the minds of the drafters of the Charter and of Secretary Stettinius in stressing the importance for peace of international cooperation in dealing with economic, social and humanitarian problems. They were not thinking, however, of *internal*—intrastate—conflict.

Today, as we consider peace-building, it is especially desirable to examine what can be achieved by functionalism in removing the causes of internal conflict. This is where functionalism—social and economic development, humanitarian assistance, institution building—has its greatest relevance, since intrastate conflict has primarily societal roots. The relationship between social justice and peace is becoming more evident and more pressing.

It is increasingly accepted, albeit conditionally at times, that intrastate conflict, if it threatens unconscionable loss of life and property, is of legitimate concern to the United Nations. Governments were for the most part loath to become involved in the genocidal conflict that engulfed Rwanda in 1994 but, in the end, they could not turn their backs.

PEACE-BUILDING AS A UNIFYING FORCE

Economic development and the protection of human rights or any of the other components of peace-building that have been mentioned are important objectives in themselves. But to view them as more than that, as elements with which to build a solid foundation for peace, provides an additional goal against which UN programs and program implementation can be assessed. Peace-building can provide a framework within which the central United Nations Organization, through the strength of its mandate for the maintenance of peace and international security, can exercise authoritative leadership in the UN system as a whole. This can do much to bring about the close coordination among the functional agencies acting in accordance with agreed priorities that, until now, has been impossible to achieve.

PEACE-BUILDING IN ACTION

Given the very breadth of peace-building, it is useful to identify specific measures in order to lend reality to the concept and appreciate what the UN has done and might do in the future. It is hardly contestable that extreme poverty, accompanied, as it usually is, by malnutrition, disease, underemployment and high birth rates, can, and too often has, contributed to social upheavals that, in turn, have led to armed domestic conflict. Many of the extensive programs initiated within the UN system over the years to promote economic development have eased these problems and thereby contributed to building a foundation for peace. But a good many—even while engendering economic growth—have not brought a notable reduction in the social and political tensions within the recipient countries. This may in some circumstances be unavoidable. More could be accomplished, however, if the various requirements for peace-building in the particular social and political circumstances of a targeted country or region are factored into the design and implementation of economic development projects, and if projects of the various functional agencies and bilateral donors are coordinated with this purpose in mind.

As an example of such an approach it is possible to think of a project for energy development in a country of varied ethnic or tribal composition. The energy project would be desirable *per se* for the economic development of the country. It could, however, have either a positive or negative effect on the social cohesion of the country. If the project is so designed as to benefit primarily one group within the country's population the results in terms of peace-building could quite possibly be negative. If, on the other hand, the project is so designed as to involve potentially conflicting population elements in its planning and implementation, and if the energy produced can be seen as of common benefit, there can be a positive, complementary gain for political and social harmony as well as economic development within the country, an objective worth achieving even if the cost of the project is thereby increased. In simple terms, economic development projects should, whenever practicable, tie the various social and political elements in a country into a network of practical cooperation and common interests.

Similarly, a complex of development projects within a region can serve to build peace among several countries if it is planned by the various UN and regional agencies, together with bilateral donors, so as to link the countries in a web of mutual economic interest and cooperative endeavor. The Mekong River project, while limited in its success because of wars having extraregional causes, still shows the potential of this approach. An integrated plan for the equitable utilization of the water resources of the Middle East (on which several agencies have worked) could have a major postconflict peace-building impact if, as now seems more likely, political circumstance permits its implementation.

Peace-building is more tangible when seen in the shorter range perspective of evident nascent crises stemming from economic or social causes within a country or region. In such circumstances the element of threat, with political as well as economic and social implications, is likely to be clear. Programs can be designed to alleviate the specific threat and resources mobilized for their realization. Again, to cite an illustrative, theoretical example: Friction between two ethnic groups in one of the poorer South Asian countries is intensified because a prolonged drought has caused great hardship among the ethnic group most heavily engaged in farming and results in a large influx of this group into the cities where the other ethnic group has traditionally been dominant. Riots ensue and the stability of the government is threatened. Carefully focused assistance programs are required to alleviate the hunger, encourage resettlement and strengthen respect for human rights if they are under threat.

This requires the same kind of system-wide coordination as longer-term assistance programs but, given the more evident humanitarian and international security implications, the UN Secretary-General is in a stronger position to take the lead in organizing coordinated action to counter the threat. The Secretary-General can bring the situation to the attention of the General Assembly (and, if the security threat is imminent, to that of the Security Council) in the expectation that the Assembly will call on agencies and governments to cooperate in a program to be organized by the Secretary-General. In such circumstances the lead can be taken by the Secretary-General, either through the designation by him of a special representative to organize the system-wide provision of the needed assistance or the designation by him of a lead agency to carry out this function in the understanding that the agency will have the continuing advice of the Secretary-General's staff.

Such a procedure is not without precedent. At the time of the African Sahel famine in the 1980s Secretary-General Pérez de Cuéllar appointed a senior member of his staff to mobilize support from member states and coordinate bilateral and multilateral emergency programs. This effort was largely successful once it got under way even though a centrally important specialized agency, the Food and Agriculture Organization, proceeded largely on its own. The UN action should have begun earlier, however, which illustrates a further need for deterrent peace-building: early warning. As was stated in Chapter 2, there is no structure through which information from the various sources within the UN system can be systematically synthesized for purposes of deterrent peace-building and preventive diplomacy. Secretary-General Boutros-Ghali suggested in his 1992 Report on the Work of the Organization that the United Nations should possess an "early warning function able to detect threats to security and well-being from energy crises to the burden of debt, from the risk of famine to the spread of disease."[5]

SOCIAL DEVELOPMENT AS PEACE-BUILDING

Like economic assistance programs, social development programs constitute an essential element in peace-building. Such social objectives as the reduction of disease, the growth of literacy, population management, and protection of the environment are so evidently linked to the development of stable societies that the introduction of political peace-building objectives in long-term planning is scarcely necessary. The priority areas for implementation of a program for the elimination of malaria, for example, will obviously be determined by the prevalence of the disease. But seeing such programs as relevant to strengthening international security can provide additional justification for the larger resources that are needed.

In the shorter term, where social tension threatens to reach critical proportions, the need to focus social development efforts to specifically reduce the likelihood of conflict becomes more evident. If abuse of human rights becomes widespread in a country, efforts to improve the situation are a needed element in peace-building. The problem that is likely to long remain for the United Nations is how to do this while respecting national sovereignty as provided in the UN Charter. As suggested earlier in a different context, one guideline should be that if a government requests assistance in strengthening respect for human rights within its territory then action by the United Nations to do so cannot infringe its sovereignty or contravene the provisions of Article 2, paragraph 7. of the Charter. Even if there is no request (and one cannot be elicited) the UN Human Rights Commission can, at the request of another state, review the situation and send a fact-finding mission or rapporteur to investigate the situation (although entry into the country would be dependent on the willingness of the government to issue visas). Such public exposure, even if on-the-spot investigation is not possible, can serve to encourage restraint on the part of the authorities and improve the prospects of peace within the society. If the abuse of human rights reaches the point where it can be justifiably considered as conflict threatening international security, stronger measures may be required. In such an eventuality the stage of peace-building would be passed and the stage of forceful intervention under Chapter VII of the Charter reached.

DEMOCRACY AND PEACE

A constant political element in peace-building is the encouragement of freedom and the strengthening of democratic forms of government. In constitutional terms this is justified by the determination expressed in the UN Charter to promote social progress and better standards of life in freedom. It is also in substantive consonance with the mandate of the UN to preserve peace, since the course of history, at least since the wars associated with the American and French revolutions, suggests that democratic governments tend not to wage war on other democratic governments. The UN has been unable to pursue this objective effectively for most of its history because of the contradictory interpretations of what freedom and democratic government mean. Still, today, the practice of democratic government remains far from universal. But democracy as an *ideology*, meaning government formed on the basis of free elections and operating under the rule of law and respect for human rights, is now widely accepted *in principle*, with the evident exception of China and the few other remaining communist governments such as Cuba and North Korea.

There is a clear majority of member states that are in favor of assistance by the UN in the holding of free elections, as evidenced by the recommendation made by the General Assembly that a special unit be established in the Secretariat to provide such service.[7] In 1992 alone the United Nations provided technical assistance for elections in Albania, the Congo, El Salvador, Ethiopia, Guinea, Guyana, Liberia, Madagascar, Mali, Rwanda, Togo and Angola. In Central America, Namibia, Cambodia and Somalia the UN has done more than monitor elections or provide technical advice. By helping to provide a stable national environment and security for elections in Nicaragua, by contributing to the drafting of the constitution in Namibia, by participating in implementation of the plan for a free, democratic government for Cambodia, and by working to restore civic institutions at the local level in Somalia, the UN has been building a basis for peace *within* those countries. As Boutros-Ghali stated in *An Agenda for Peace*, "There is an obvious connection between democratic practices—such as the rule of law and transparency in decision making—and the achievement of true peace and security in any new and stable political order. These elements of good governance need to be promoted at all levels of international and national political communities."

This type of political peace-building has until now been carried out largely in postconflict situations. However, as suggested in the earlier chapter on peacekeeping, the UN should be in a position to assist member states in the strengthening of democratic processes, on their request, in circumstances of internal tension prior to its escalation to armed combat. This is a prime example of a peace-building measure that the United

Nations can now take—albeit with much discretion—that was not possible
during the Cold War period.

THE ROLE OF ECOSOC

Peace-building clearly calls for greater coordination of program planning
and resource application not only among UN functional agencies, but
also among national donors of bilateral aid. There needs to be an integrated approach to the objectives of peace, democracy and human rights
and the requirements of development.[8] The UN, as an institution, needs
to be in a stronger position to give strategic direction to both multilateral
and bilateral assistance programs. Further, a system needs to be developed through which the political and social dimensions can be more fully
reflected in economic planning.

There is a longstanding understanding between the United Nations Organization and the World Bank that the UN will not make recommendations
to the Bank on loans. It is sound policy that World Bank loans should not be
subject to majority decision by the General Assembly. This should not exclude,
however, close consultation between the UN and the financial institutions in
the establishment of priorities and the design of programs that are intended
to build a foundation for peace in a particular country. If economic structural
reform programs and programs to strengthen democratic institutions are
pursued by separate UN agencies without integration at the planning stage
their common objective of enhancing human security can be seriously jeopardized. This has unfortunately been the case in El Salvador. Alvaro de Soto,
the UN Mediator in the Salvadoran peace process, and Graciana del Castillo,
a Secretariat economic officer, have written that "the IMF and the World Bank
did not involve the United Nations in the elaboration of the economic
stabilization *cum* structural adjustment programme. Similarly, when the
United Nations became engaged in the negotiating process in 1990, it did not
consult the IMF or the Bank, notwithstanding the serious financial implications which it would entail. . . . The United Nations, the IMF and the Bank did
not operate as if they formed part of the same system, but rather as if they
were functioning in separate worlds."[9] A system must be devised that will
preclude such uncoordinated approaches to building peace.

In examining how the peace-building function can be better performed by
the United Nations a number of considerations have to be kept in mind. The
Economic and Social Council, which now consists of fifty-four member states,
may, according to the Charter, coordinate the activities of the specialized
agencies through consultation with, and recommendations to, such agencies,
and through recommendations to the General Assembly and to the members
of the United Nations. Moreover, "It may make arrangements with the
Members of the United Nations and with the specialized agencies to obtain

reports on the steps taken to give effect to its own recommendations and to recommendations on matters falling within its competence made by the General Assembly."[10] Thus ECOSOC is endowed with the threefold responsibility of policy formulation, program coordination and the monitoring of policy implementation. These responsibilities are of central importance to the success of the United Nations in building peace. But lacking any real source of power or of credibility in the formulation of global policies, ECOSOC has not, until now, been able to fulfill these functions.

The Secretary-General of the United Nations has no authority over the specialized agencies and no control over their programs. An Administrative Committee for Coordination (ACC) was established by ECOSOC to facilitate cooperation among the agencies and functional offices. The Secretary-General serves as permanent chairman, thus assuming the status of *primus inter pares*, but this does not translate into any power beyond that of persuasion. Thus, there has never been in the United Nations an effective means of synthesizing the programs of the functional offices and agencies in pursuit of commonly agreed upon priority objectives determined on the basis of political as well as economic and social considerations. For peace-building purposes this void needs to be filled. The most direct way of achieving this might seem to be to centralize control of program formulation of the specialized agencies, including the financial institutions, in the UN General Assembly, with the UN Secretary-General accorded supervisory status over the heads of these agencies. This would run directly counter to the intentions of the founders of the UN.

Centralization of control was deliberately avoided as giving the central UN organization too much power and as permitting the intrusion of political disputes—with which the General Assembly and the Security Council would inevitably be concerned—that would disrupt the work of the functional agencies. Moreover, it was considered that the central UN organs would not have the expertise or the time to deal with the technical subjects with which the functional agencies would be concerned. These considerations are still valid. The General Assembly is not well suited to exercise supervisory control over the specialized agencies. Moreover, any such plan would encounter such strong opposition from the specialized agencies and from Member States as to render it unworkable. Nonetheless, greater guidance from the central UN Organization, which is concerned with political as well as social and economic factors, is needed for peace-building. An invigorated ECOSOC, if it enjoyed the greater authority that can come from the commitment of member states, could meet this need at least in part without requiring a change in the Charter or departing from its original intent. Acting under instructions from ECOSOC the Secretary-General could serve as its agent in exercising a degree of supervision over the specialized agencies.

A start has been made in this direction. In 1991 the decision was made that ECOSOC would have only one session annually instead of two as had been the case until then. This was intended as part of the restructuring and revitalization process of the United Nations in the economic, social and related fields that *inter alia* would enable the Economic and Social Council to enhance "its role as a central forum for major economic, social and related issues and policies and for coordinating functions related to the United Nations system." [11] A specific objective is to pursue "an integrated approach to policy and programme aspects of the economic and social issues." At its 1992 substantive session the Council declared that objectives of securing peace, development and justice were indivisible and equally essential. The Council reiterated that international development cooperation and the eradication of poverty were inextricably linked with the preservation of peace.

With only one annual session, greater discipline is required in formulating the agenda. Four or five days of each session are to be devoted "to the coordination of the policies and activities of the specialized agencies, organs, organizations and bodies of the United Nations system relating to the achievement of the economic and social objectives of the United Nations."[12] The annual session now includes a "high level segment" of four days with ministerial participation as well as the participation of the heads of the relevant UN functional agencies and offices.

Thus some response has been made to the need for a more authoritative ECOSOC and for greater ECOSOC effectiveness in coordinating the activities of the various functional elements in the UN system. For his part, the Secretary-General has sought to play a stronger leadership role in the Administrative Coordination Committee (ACC) and met considerable resistance from some of the Specialized Agency heads in the process. However, the steps taken are patently far from adequate to enable ECOSOC to give central leadership and direction for either the policy formulation or program integration needed for peace-building. Notably, the General Assembly resolution that defines the changes made in ECOSOC speaks only of the revitalization of the United Nations in the economic, social and related fields. No mention is made of international security in this context, or of peace-building.

Secretary-General Boutros-Ghali recognized that ECOSOC could hardly provide effective, continuing coordination of UN programs in the economic and social fields that is vital for peace-building if it were not in session for the greater part of the year. He therefore suggested, in addressing the high level segment in 1992, that "a flexible high-level inter-sessional mechanism" be introduced "in order to facilitate a timely response to evolving socio-economic realities." Such a mechanism, he said, "would enable the Council to play a central monitoring and surveillance role within the United Nations."[13] Some such standing body competent to deal with economic and social problems affecting international security on a continuing basis is

essential if the United Nations is to fulfill the requirements of peace-building into the next century. Governments did not respond, however, to the
Secretary-General's recommendation.

The authority that an enhanced ECOSOC will need to fulfill the role
foreseen for it in peace-building will depend on the following conditions:

- The willingness of member states to regard it as the principal forum
  for global policy formulation;

- The readiness of member states, as members of the Specialized
  Agencies, including the financial institutions, to accord ECOSOC
  clear responsibility to coordinate the programs of the system;

- The ability of the Secretary-General or the senior Secretariat officials in the economic and social areas to provide intellectual stimu-
  lus in the formulation of global policies;

- The success of the structural reform of ECOSOC and the economic
  and social areas of the United Nations;

- Development of a close working relationship between ECOSOC
  and the Security Council that will recognize the direct relationship
  between economic and social developments and international
  security.

THE COMPETENCE OF THE SECURITY COUNCIL

Under the UN Charter, the Security Council is given primary responsibility for the maintenance of peace and international security. This has been
interpreted until now as a political responsibility. The Council has never
dealt with economic and social issues *per se*. The Economic and Social
Council reports to the General Assembly, not to the Security Council. Since
economic and social developments increasingly influence the maintenance
of international security, the question inevitably arises as to the degree—if
at all—the mandate of the Security Council extends to these fields. How can
the Security Council meet its responsibility to prevent war if it has no
control or influence on social and economic developments? At least a partial
answer is provided in the Charter which states that the Economic and Social
Council may furnish information to the Security Council and "shall assist
the Security Council on its request."[14] It was thus foreseen from the beginning that the Security Council might, in pursuit of its mandate, interest itself
in economic and social matters. This the Council has not done. But it will
need to do so if conflict is to be avoided in the coming years.

For this purpose, the Security Council and ECOSOC should develop a
procedure for liaison and orderly consultation that takes into account their
mutual objective of maintaining international security and building peace,

and their respective capacities to act. With regard to the latter, there is a distinctive difference between the Security Council and ECOSOC. Under Article 25 of the Charter member states commit themselves to accept and carry out the decisions of the Security Council. Its decisions relating to the maintenance of international security and peace are therefore binding in principle on all UN Members. ECOSOC may only make recommendations. This it can do to the General Assembly, to states and to the specialized agencies. It is reasonable to expect ECOSOC to take security considerations into account in recommending policies and actions to the appropriate governmental and/or nongovernmental actors with the objective of building peace and to be responsible for coordinating and monitoring their implementation.

The Security Council, in turn, should have knowledge of, and take into account, economic and social developments in determining action to be taken to maintain and strengthen international security. The Security Council would have responsibility to take *enforcement* action pertaining to such developments should they constitute a threat to international security. It might, for example, call on a government to desist from an action such as massive violation of human rights amounting to genocide. It could impose sanctions in the event of noncompliance with treaty obligations concerning nuclear or chemical or bacteriological weapons, or protection of the global environment. Secretary-General Boutros-Ghali has suggested that the Secretary-General and the UN human rights bodies be empowered to bring massive violations of human rights to the attention of the Security Council, together with recommendations for action.[15]

In order to ensure that economic and social issues are fully taken into account in the context of peace-building by the competent organ or organs of the UN, an interdisciplinary analysis and planning staff should be established under the Secretary-General. Such a staff should include experts in economic and social development as well as in political affairs and should have access to information relevant to international security (including its economic and social dimensions) flowing in from the various departments of the Secretariat and from the functional offices and agencies of the UN system. It would be the function of this staff to analyze developments in terms of their potential affect on international security and to formulate suggestions for action by the various elements of the UN system in order to strengthen the basis for peace wherever peace might be in danger. The analysis and planning staff would provide the Secretary-General with its conclusions and recommendations and the Secretary-General could on this basis put forward suggestions for action by ECOSOC or the Security Council or both. The staff would serve as the primary synthesizing instrument for bringing together the various factors that need to be taken into account for peace-building.

To recapitulate, peace-building is an undertaking that must engage at some stage all parts of the United Nations system as well as governments, regional and nongovernmental organizations. In such a broad endeavor effective leadership is of paramount importance. The United Nations is the only organization with a mandate broad enough for this role. Secretary-General Boutros-Ghali has made an energetic, sometimes abrasive, effort to exercise such leadership, both personally and as chief administrative officer of the United Nations. To endow the United Nations with the necessary leadership authority, however, a more fundamental reform of the economic and social sectors of the UN system than has yet been undertaken will be needed. Only through such a process can ECOSOC, or a successor economic security organ, and the Secretary-General gain the authority to establish the policies and priorities that will guide the relevant activities of all of the functional offices and agencies of the system. Resources will never be adequate to allow the luxury of duplication. This means greater central management, and with it the ability to ensure that the resources available to the UN system serve ultimately to strengthen the basis for peace.

Fundamental reform of this nature will be strongly resisted by the executive heads of some, if not all, functional agencies. It can only be effected if member states—who, after all, exercise control over the agencies, exert the necessary pressure. The countries of the North and the South will have to work together. It may just be that the new opportunities for peace-building in the post-Cold War era will persuade them to do so and provide the spur for such a restructuring of the UN system.

NOTES

1. See Immanuel Kant, "Eternal Peace," in *The Philosophy of Kant* (The Modern Library, 1949) for consideration of the relationship between "republican" government and peace.

2. Javier Pérez de Cuéllar, *Anarchy or Order* (New York: United Nations, 1991), pp. 341–42.

3. Edward R. Stettinius, Jr., *Report to the President on the San Francisco Conference*. Department of State, 26 June 1945.

4. Inis Claude, *Swords into Plowshares*, chapter 17 (New York: Random House, 1984).

5. UN Document A/47/1, par. 71, 11 September 1993.

6. Cf. Bruce Russett, *Grasping the Democratic Peace* (Princeton, N.J.: Princeton University Press, 1993).

7. See GA Resolution 46/137, 17 December 1991.

8. Ibid., par. 67.

9. Alvarao de Soto and Graciana del Castillo, "Obstacles to Peace-building," *Foreign Policy*, Spring, 1993, pp. 69–83.

10. UN Charter, Articles 63 and 64.

11. See General Assembly Resolution A/RES/45/264, 30 May 1991.

12. Report of the Secretary-General on the Work of the Organization. A/47/1, 11 September 1992, p. 22.

13. Ibid., p. 23.

14. UN Charter, Article 65.

15. UN Document A/47/1, par. 101, 11 September 1992.

6

Enhancing Nuclear Security in a Multipolar World

One of the many happy results of the end of the Cold War was the practical elimination of the fear of a catastrophic nuclear conflict between the two major nuclear powers, a fear that had held a whole generation in trauma. Ironically, it is the nuclear weapons of these two powers (the USSR having now been replaced by Russia) that have been under the most extensive and reliable mutual safeguards. The United States and the USSR had in place alert centers that, while staffed unilaterally, assured immediate communication between the two countries with regard to any apparent nuclear launching or action that might be interpreted as such. The centers continue to function with Russia taking the place of the USSR. Moreover, the United States and Russia have highly sophisticated (and expensive) control systems, with which they are mutually familiar, that make accidental or unauthorized nuclear launchings practically impossible. This provides a basis for confidence between the two powers, offering assurance against counterlaunching, or the triggering and automatic escalation of alert systems in response to actions of nonhostile intent.

The agreements reached between the United States and the USSR/Russia on the reduction of their nuclear arsenals should further stabilize their security relationship. However, the alert and safeguard arrangements and understandings that exist between the United States and Russia are bilateral. Belorus, Ukraine and Kazakhstan continue to have nuclear weapons of the former Soviet Union on their territory. They are under central, unified control within the framework of the Commonwealth of Independent States (CIS) and are believed to be encompassed in the U.S.\Russian arrangements. It is unclear, however, how effective the central control is or how long it will last. Belorus is fully committed to becoming a nonnuclear weapons state. On the other hand, Ukraine (until recently) and Kazakhstan have at times shown an inclination to maintain an independent, national nuclear capacity.

Hotline facilities exist between France and Russia and the UK and Russia but these do not involve the constant presence of experts able to interpret nuclear-related events and maintain the continuing contact that could help to avoid any misinterpretation.

OUTSIDE THE NUCLEAR NETWORK

The other nuclear power, China, is not included in any alert network. Neither, of course, are the several countries with a known or suspected capacity to produce nuclear weapons and launch systems. Located as a number of them are in volatile regions, nuclear activity in any one of them that might be interpreted as a nuclear launching or preparations for such could lead to catastrophic consequences unless subject to immediate (or even better, prior) clarification. The discovery of Iraq's nuclear weapon and delivery system development programs and the acknowledgement by South Africa that it had developed a modest nuclear weapons capacity (now happily destroyed) lends frightening reality to this prospect. The suspected nuclear weapons programs in North Korea, Pakistan, India and Israel illustrate the extent to which potential danger spots are outside of any alert network. If Kazakhstan decides to maintain a national nuclear capacity outside of CIS—effectively Russian—control, an additional acknowledged nuclear power will be outside of any alert system. There is, moreover, the danger that countries without the domestic capacity to produce nuclear weapons might be able to purchase the various components and seek to gain in this way a onetime nuclear capacity. Iraq was able to purchase critical parts for its nuclear weapons development from Western countries. With the collapse of the Soviet internal security system, and the spread of chaotic economic conditions in the former Soviet republics, the possibility of illegal sales of nuclear weapons components has become even greater. Under these circumstances there is also a greater possibility that irresponsible elements can gain access to a nuclear device and seek to use it to gain their ends by terror. Thus, the reality is that in the post–Cold War period the threat posed by the existence of real or potential nuclear capacities outside of any international system of control or alerts has grown rather than decreased. The problem exceeds the possibilities of bilateral management. A multilateral approach is required.

The most effective means to eliminate the threat to international security posed by nuclear weapons would obviously be the complete elimination of such weapons and universal accession to the Non-Proliferation Treaty. Neither is likely to occur very soon. There are ways, however, of limiting the danger of an unintentional nuclear exchange, of bringing countries together in common defense against irresponsible resort to nuclear weapons by governments or terrorist groups and of lessening the sense of insecurity that can prompt a country to pursue the nuclear option.

The first requirement is to achieve the greatest possible transparency with regard to developments of military significance in the nuclear field, a transparency that would make information on such developments available to all countries, whether they have sophisticated national means of intelligence or not. Transparency can serve to reassure nonnuclear weapons states that they are well-informed of the conditions they face and encourage cooperation in dealing with any threat that arises. It can serve, too, to deter a government from going nuclear by exposing it to pressure and condemnation.

The second requirement is the means for instantaneous interchange of information on any threatening nuclear event among all affected parties.

The third requirement is a forum in which nonnuclear states can participate in managing the nuclear threat in order to reduce their sense of exclusion from the nuclear club.

Finally, a permanent organization is needed to advise the Security Council on nuclear weapons developments and to undertake fact-finding and monitoring at the Council's request.

The establishment by the United Nations of a multilateral nuclear alert center would serve these purposes.[1]

THE OBJECTIVES OF A MULTILATERAL NUCLEAR ALERT CENTER

With the overall objective of enhancing international security by reducing the risk of nuclear war and discouraging further proliferation, a nuclear alert center would provide states with a constant source of information, warning and clarification, and a permanent point of contact on nuclear events of military significance.

Specifically the center should be organized to

- Receive and assess information from all available sources, including national intelligence satellites, on indications of unusual or threatening nuclear activity. Participating governments would undertake to provide relevant information to the center just as they do to the International Atomic Energy Agency (IAEA) concerning

the possible diversion of nuclear fuel intended for peaceful purposes.

- Obtain on a continuing basis information from the IAEA on any
  diversion of nuclear fuel and seek to clarify for what purpose the
  diversion has been perpetrated.

- Seek immediate clarification through expert analysis and intergovernmental consultation of any threatening nuclear event and
  provide instantaneous notification to all affected parties.

- Inform the UN Secretary-General, the Security Council and Member States (as needed by the urgency of the situation) of nuclear
  developments affecting international security, with assessment of
  their implications and advice on appropriate countermeasures if
  indicated.

- Develop a data bank on nuclear arms, nuclear capacities and
  nuclear components (including their sale) that would be of assistance in interpreting incoming reports on known or suspected
  activities related to nuclear weapons.

- Dispatch, at the direction of the Security Council, fact-finding
  teams for on-the-spot investigation of reports of suspicious nuclear
  activity.

- Monitor compliance with treaties on the reduction or limitation of
  nuclear weapons, should the United Nations be given this responsibility in the future.

With instantaneous communication capacity and continuing contact
with many states, the center could counter, through quick, informed clarification, misinterpretation of a nuclear event that could activate alert systems and lead to nuclear war. It could serve as an important
confidence-building instrumentality encompassing both nuclear and nonnuclear states. Further, by providing a forum in which nonnuclear states
could participate on the same basis as nuclear weapons states in the
monitoring of military nuclear developments, a center could reduce the
sense of discrimination felt by many nonnuclear weapons countries. By
serving as a point of clarification and exchange regarding reports of nuclear
weapons development in individual states the center could reduce pressure
for competitive proliferation.

STRUCTURE AND ORGANIZATION

A multilateral nuclear alert center, as envisioned here, could consist of
two parts: a) a permanent staff made up of technically qualified interna-

tional civil servants (some seconded from governments for this duty); and b) an intergovernmental consultative council that would meet regularly, and on an *ad hoc* basis as required, to review developments, consider reports and analyses provided by the center staff, and give guidance on the center's operation. The Council would be made up of qualified representatives of the five nuclear weapons states and of a limited number of nonnuclear states. The latter would rotate on an established schedule, such as every three years.

A multilateral nuclear alert center could be established by decision of the General Assembly on recommendation of the Security Council as part of the United Nations Organization or, alternatively, by an international conference as a semi-independent agency closely linked to the United Nations but with its own budget and financial support, having a status similar to that of the IAEA. The direct relevance of the purposes of the center to the maintenance of international security would suggest that establishment as part of the UN Organization would be the more appropriate. In either event, a center could best be physically located in Vienna in proximity to the IAEA with which it would need to work in close cooperation.

A center would have to have an advanced communications system, giving it instantaneous access to the UN Secretary-General, the Security Council, and the capitals of participating states. Information and analyses would be exchanged on a regular basis with United Nations Headquarters.

In a monitoring role, the center could not be expected to have the resources to set up an independent global watch to detect the movement of nuclear weapons or weapons components. It would be heavily dependent on information provided by other intergovernmental organizations and nongovernmental organizations and from national governments. The expectation of this type of cooperation by member states would be one of the premises on which the center would be founded.

NUCLEAR SECURITY IN THE POST–COLD WAR WORLD

A nuclear alert center could, through its functions, contribute directly to the strengthening of security in the post–Cold War era. In addition it could provide vital support to the Security Council as it seeks to fulfill its broadening security responsibilities. Since the end of the Cold War the Security Council, on the basis of its security mandate and of the provisions of the Non-Proliferation Treaty, has begun to take action to prevent the spread of nuclear weapons. In its resolution, setting the terms for a cease-fire in the Gulf War,[2] the Council demanded that Iraq unconditionally agree not to acquire or develop nuclear weapons or nuclear-weapons-usable material and place any that it had under exclusive control of the IAEA. Subsequently, the statement issued by the Council on the occasion of its summit level meeting in January 1992[3] contained a paragraph indicating that the Council intended to take appropriate measures in the case of any violations of the Non-Proliferation Treaty (NPT) by signatory states. When, in the spring of 1993, it was notified by the IAEA that North Korea had violated provisions of the safeguards agreement it had signed with the IAEA, the Security Council adopted a resolution calling on North Korea to abide fully with its obligations and suggesting that the Council would consider further measures if this did not happen. The Council further urged North Korea to reconsider its decision to withdraw from the NPT.[4]

Given the broad agreement that exists in the Security Council, particularly among the five permanent members, on the dangers posed by nuclear weapons in the hands of irresponsible governments or groups,[5] it seems reasonable to expect that the Council will take action in the future to curb a serious nuclear threat even if it does not constitute a violation of the NPT. A nuclear alert center as described in this chapter could become a vital adjunct to the Council in this context. The IAEA has the responsibility to monitor nuclear facilities intended for peaceful purposes and is obligated to inform the Security Council, as it did in the North Korean case, of any noncompliance with safeguard agreements pertaining to such facilities. The IAEA, however, does not have a mandate to monitor nuclear developments in the military field nor is it equipped to carry out the functions of a nuclear alert center as they have been defined in this chapter.

The IAEA and a UN nuclear alert center can be seen as mutually complementary, serving together purposes of vital importance in preventing the spread of nuclear capacity, the possibility of unintentional nuclear exchange and access by irresponsible elements to nuclear weapons. A multilateral nuclear alert center could, in conjunction with the IAEA, contribute to the building of confidence among states in the vastly different circumstances of the post–Cold War era.

NOTES

1. The establishment of a nuclear alert center was first proposed in the 1986 Annual Report of Secretary-General Pérez de Cuéllar to the General Assembly. The report is contained in *Anarchy or Order, Annual Reports 1982–1991* (New York: United Nations, 1991), p. 117.

2. Security Council Resolution 687, 3 April 1991.

3. Security Council Document S/23500, 31 January 1992.

4. Security Council Resolution 825, 11 May 1993.

5. China, despite its close relationship with North Korea, abstained on the resolution insisting that North Korea comply with its safeguards agreement, thus permitting its adoption.

7

The Potential of
Regional Organizations

In speaking of the maintenance of international security, Winston Churchill once proclaimed that "there should be several regional councils, august, but subordinate; these should form the massive pillars upon which the world organization would be founded in majesty and calm."[1] This is perhaps the most flamboyant statement of that school of thought that attributed very high importance to the role of regional organizations in maintaining peace. At the San Francisco Conference, when the United Nations was founded, there was strong support for this approach. Those countries already committed to regional arrangements—the Commonwealth, the Inter-American system, the Arab League—insisted that adequate provision be made in the UN Charter for effective regional participation in the preservation of peace. The Latin Americans objected to the veto power of the permanent members of the Security Council on the ground that it could jeopardize the authority and cohesion of regional organizations. Australia along with Belgium and Venezuela proposed to "qualify" the veto in the case of regional enforcement action.

The United States, pressed by the Latin American countries, supported recognition in the Charter of the role of regional organizations. At the same time, however, the Americans were wary of the regionalist approach, reflecting a continuing Wilsonian tendency to identify regionalism with competitive alliances. Secretary of State Stettinius reported to President

Truman that concessions to regionalist pressures should not establish "a precedent which might engender rivalry between regional groups at the expense of world security."[2]

What emerged in the Charter is, as was necessary, a compromise. The Charter, according to Inis Claude, "conferred general approval upon existing and anticipated regional organizations, but contained provisions having the purpose of making them serve as adjuncts to the United Nations and subjecting them in considerable measure to the direction and control of the central organization."

The course of history since San Francisco has led neither to regional organizations that would be pillars of the UN, in Churchill's phrase, nor to a UN intent on dominating, directing, or even using regional organizations for purposes of international security. The cooperation between the United Nations and regional organizations on security problems has, for most of the years since 1945, been tenuous at best. However, as the United Nations has assumed ever greater responsibility in dealing with regional conflicts in the post–Cold War era, it has looked more to the regional organizations as potential partners, only to experience until now profound disappointment. Regional organizations, for their part, have recognized the need for the UN to be active—even dominant—in handling regional disputes.

The number and range of what are broadly referred to as regional organizations are very large. NATO, the Arab League, CARICOM all can be categorized under this heading, although not necessarily as coming within the purview of Chapter VIII of the UN Charter that defines the relationship between the UN and "regional arrangements." Regional organizations can be concerned primarily with economic cooperation, mutual security, political coordination or a combination of these and other concerns. For present purposes regional arrangements can be defined as intergovernmental in nature—this is certainly the assumption of the Charter. A regional arrangement or agency, then, is an organization in which governments from a defined region or with a close connection to the region are joined for commonly agreed purposes.

The UN Charter is not concerned with all regional organizations; rather, only those dealing "with such matters relating to the maintenance of international peace and security as are appropriate for regional action." There is no objection to UN members joining such organizations provided "they are consistent with the Purposes and Principles of the United Nations."

Most if not all of the regional organizations that fit into this category include some form of commitment to these purposes and principles in their charters. The North Atlantic Treaty, for example, commits its parties to conform to the rules of international behavior laid down in the UN Charter, provides that NATO activities will be conducted within the authorization and limitations prescribed in Article 51 of the Charter, and disavows any intent to revise the rights or duties of parties that are members of the United Nations or to infringe upon the established responsibilities of the Security Council.[3]

THE CONSTITUTIONAL RELATIONSHIP BETWEEN THE UN AND REGIONAL ORGANIZATIONS

Chapter VIII of the UN Charter suggests that local disputes should be settled in the first instance through regional arrangements "either at the initiative of the states concerned or by reference from the Security Council." The prerogative of the Security Council is preserved to investigate any dispute, as is the right of any state to bring a dispute directly to the Security Council or the General Assembly. No enforcement action is to be taken by a regional organization without the authorization of the Security Council, but the Security Council *"shall where appropriate, utilize such regional arrangements or agencies for enforcement action under its authority."* The Security Council had never resorted to this until the Bosnian conflict. In seeking to halt Bosnian Serb attacks on "safe areas," the Security Council, as we have seen, decided that "Member States, acting nationally or through regional organizations or arrangements, may take . . . all necessary measures, through the use of air power, in and around the safe areas in the Republic of Bosnia and Herzegovina, to support UNPROFOR in the performance of its mandate." This mandate was "to deter attacks against the safe areas, to monitor the cease-fire, to promote the withdrawal of military and paramilitary units other than those of the Government of the Republic of Bosnia and Herzegovina and to occupy some key points on the ground, in addition to participating in the delivery of humanitarian relief."[4] The intent was to utilize NATO for enforcement purposes even though NATO was not named.

Formal agreements exist between the UN and a number of regional organizations including the OAU, the League of Arab States, and the Organization of the Islamic Conference defining their relationship. The agreements with the regional organizations provide for cooperation in general terms, but they do not contain provisions governing the handling of regional disputes or the exchange of information relative to international security. An agreement was negotiated between the OAS and the UN but has not been signed. The CSCE declared in 1992 that it was a regional arrangement within the meaning of Chapter VIII of the Charter. All of these organizations now have observer status with the UN, as does the European Union.

THE PERFORMANCE OF REGIONAL ORGANIZATIONS IN
SECURITY MATTERS

From one perspective the primarily internal nature of most regional conflicts would suggest that regional organizations are best suited to resolve them. The regional organizations should be more familiar with the root causes; their intervention would seem less "foreign"; their peacekeepers might seem more readily acceptable to the people involved if they shared a similar culture and language. On the basis of recent experience, however, rather the contrary is the case. The dominant role of the UN in dealing with most regional disputes is evident, for example, in the Western Sahara, Cambodia, the Persian Gulf, Afghanistan, Angola, Nicaragua, Haiti, Mozambique, Somalia, Rwanda and the former Yugoslavia. The only regional conflict that has been primarily handled by a regional organization is the civil war in Liberia where the course of events has illustrated the dangers of this option as well as its potential. Even there the UN has been given, at a late stage, a prominent role in peacemaking, although it has not provided a peace-keeping force.

Of the regional organizations only the Organization of American States (OAS) has had notable success in the resolution of regional disputes without the participation of the UN. These include conflicts between Costa Rica and Nicaragua (1948–49, 1955–56, 1959), Honduras and Nicaragua (1957), Venezuela and the Dominican Republic (1960–61), Venezuela and Cuba (1963–64, 1967), the Dominican Republic and Haiti (1950, 1963–65), Panama and the U.S. (1964), and El Salvador and Honduras (1960–70). These "solo" achievements ended a quarter of a century ago. This can be attributed to the increasing intrusion of the Cold War into the region; declining homogeneity as a result of the advent of more English-speaking Caribbean countries; increased dissatisfaction with U.S. policy orientation and U.S. dominance of the organization; and finally, the declining enthusiasm of the U.S., itself, for the OAS. With the end of the Cold War, the ideological tension within the region declined substantially and the OAS, with encouragement from the UN, has become more engaged in dealing with regional conflicts. However, the major initiatives for peace in Central America have been taken by *ad hoc* groups such as Contadora.

The Association of Southeast Asian Nations (ASEAN) was founded with the primary goal of assuring regional peace and security. Its members called for "collective political defense" to protect individual as well as group interests. The concept of military defense was intentionally avoided. An *ad hoc* body of mediators was established as a legal mechanism for the peaceful settlement of disputes. ASEAN members are legally bound to seek its help before turning elsewhere for assistance in the event of a dispute. Members have so far not needed to make use of this facility. ASEAN aided in bringing the parties together to end the Cambodian conflict. It worked in coordina-

tion with the UN, which ultimately assumed the major role in the development and implementation of the peace plan for the country (greatly facilitated by the permanent members of the Security Council). ASEAN efforts
on Cambodia brought greater political solidarity to the association and
made of it a stronger regional organization with enhanced potential.

The efforts of the Organization of African Unity (OAU) at peacemaking
and peacekeeping have been singularly unsuccessful. Its experience in
Chad and the Western Sahara demonstrated that alone it has neither the
resources nor the internal cohesion to successfully undertake peacemaking
or peacekeeping within the region. Significantly, it played no role in the
Liberian conflict, nor in resolving the conflicts in southern Africa that
preceded Namibia's transition to independence.

In June 1983, the OAU, "against the background of many prolonged and
destructive conflicts on our continent and of our limited success at finding
lasting solutions to them," established a Mechanism for Conflict Prevention, Management and Resolution. The Mechanism has as a primary objective the anticipation and prevention of conflicts. In circumstances where
conflicts have occurred it will be its responsibility to undertake peace-making and peace-building functions. If conflicts "degenerate to the extent of
requiring collective international intervention and policing, the assistance
or, where appropriate, the services of the United Nations will be sought."[5]

When asked by the UN Secretary-General to assume responsibility for
peacekeeping in Rwanda, the OAU declined on the ground that the UN was
better equipped to do it. The OAU is only able to deploy small observer
groups (as it did in Rwanda when the first peace agreement was reached).
Involvement in intrastate conflict also poses a problem for the organization.
The OAU Secretary-General dealt with this issue head-on when he addressed the first meeting of the Conflict Prevention Mechanism. Assuming
that the OAU was prepared in principle to intervene in such conflicts, he
proposed that members determine whether an identical approach should
be taken to all categories of internal conflict: "those arising from the process
of democratization, those that are ethnically based, or those that are religious in nature."[6] While this question has not been answered, it is significant
that OAU members are willing to give formal consideration to the highly
sensitive subject of intervention in internal conflicts.

The League of Arab States and the Organization of the Islamic Conference have been no more successful than the OAU in dealing with regional
conflict. Both sought to resolve the Iran/Iraq war with no success. The Arab
Deterrent Force that was deployed in Lebanon was not strictly speaking a
League undertaking (having been initiated solely by Syria) and was in any
event hardly a success. With the Iraqi invasion of Kuwait the League was
not only impotent, it split as a result of internal pressures, a repetition of its
earlier experience at the time of Egypt's peace with Israel.

In considering the performance of regional organizations it is now necessary also to include the Commonwealth of Independent States (CIS), which incorporates Asian as well as European states. The CIS applied for, and was granted, observer status at the UN as a regional organization as defined in Chapter VIII of the Charter. It has undertaken peace-keeping actions to some effect in several of the new states that emerged from the disintegration of the Soviet Union. The CIS peace-keeping forces are quite different from those organized by the UN since they are composed almost entirely of Russian troops and are commanded by Russian officers. They are deployed in countries in which Russia has so direct an interest as to raise questions concerning the impartiality of the CIS forces in dealing with civil conflicts, in most of which leaders of the former Soviet Union are involved. Russia has requested that the United Nations endorse and provide financial support for the CIS peace-keeping operations. The United Nations hesitated, not wishing to authorize action that might prove inconsistent with the UN Charter. However, the Security Council eventually endorsed the CIS operations as legitimate peacekeeping. The UN did not extend financial support.

As a regional organization the CIS is inevitably dominated by Russia. Russia contends that it bears special responsibility for the security of the former republics of the Soviet Union. In the words of Russian Foreign Minister Kozyrev, "Russia cannot pull out of Abkhazia or Tajikistan the way America did from Somalia." He insists that "Russia's peacekeeping mission . . . acts in complete accordance with international law and at the request of the states concerned. But the cooperation of the world community, including the use of international observers and material support, is of great value."[7] It has to be acknowledged that for the vast territory of the former Soviet Union there is now a regional organization that, while short on financial resources, has available the troops, equipment and command and control procedures that are needed for peacekeeping and peace-enforcement.

EUROPEAN REGIONAL ORGANIZATIONS AND THE YUGOSLAV CRISIS

There was a wide inclination to think of the European Community (now the European Union) as the center of economic power in Europe, the Conference on Security and Cooperation in Europe as the arbiter of human and democratic rights, and the North Atlantic Treaty Organization as the military guarantor of peace and stability. The events in Yugoslavia have shown that this neat categorization is not valid or useful in the face of internal ethnic strife that amounts to civil war.

The CSCE, the European Community, NATO and the Western European Union (WE) all became engaged in efforts to end hostilities in Yugoslavia, the first time any of them had sought to end armed conflict in the interest of regional security. Their performance is indicative of the limitations of even the best organized and wealthiest of regional arrangements. If there is hope of placing greater reliance on the regional organizations in the future, it is important to understand why, with the exception of NATO, they have had such little success. The comparative roles of the UN and the European regional organizations in Croatia and Bosnia are particularly instructive in this respect.

The CSCE clearly meets the criteria for a regional organization as defined in the UN Charter. Commitment to the purposes and principles of the United Nations Charter is a prominent feature of the Helsinki Final Act. The Final Act refers to cooperation with the UN in a number of specific fields, albeit not in that of security. This commitment is repeated in the "Charter of Paris for a New Europe" adopted at the CSCE Summit Meeting in November, 1990.[8] In the "Charter" the participants recognized "with satisfaction the growing role of the United Nations in world affairs and its increasing effectiveness, fostered by the improvement in relations among our States." A decision was taken at the meeting to establish a "Conflict Prevention Centre" to assist the CSCE Council in reducing the risk of war. It was stated that initially the Centre's role would consist of giving support to the implementation of confidence and security-building measures (CSBMs), but this was without prejudice to the possibility that the Centre might assume additional tasks related to dispute settlement and conciliation. The Centre has since been given the additional task of providing early warning for the CSCE High Commissioner for the Protection of Minorities.

Secretary-General Pérez de Cuéllar, in addressing the CSCE Summit, said that he perceived "major opportunities" for cooperation between the United Nations and CSCE on matters of common concern. The first matter that he listed was the prevention and resolution of conflicts. The Secretary-General did not suggest—although he would have been well-advised to do so—any way in which this cooperation might be formalized or structured.

When the first meeting of the CSCE Council was held in Berlin in June 1991, German Chancellor Kohl stated that the "shared responsibility of the CSCE countries requires that we now create . . . a pan-European security architecture within the CSCE framework." "The new European architecture," he said, "must be built on the foundations that have brought about . . . the transformation throughout Europe: the CSCE process, the Council of Europe, the European Community, the Atlantic Alliance, and the disarmament and arms control process."[9] Again, no mention was made of the UN. This was—until Yugoslavia—the consistent trend in CSCE deliberations and documents relating to security.

The CSCE has, as its title implies, the mandate to encourage security and cooperation in all of Europe. Yugoslavia was a charter CSCE member. When Yugoslavia broke apart and conflict erupted in Croatia, the CSCE seemed the most appropriate organization to step in, bring an end to the fighting and work toward a resolution of this eminently European problem. It was quickly seized of the conflict and, almost as quickly, proved incapable of effective action. First, the CSCE functions on the basis of consensus and there was no consensus on the action it might take in Yugoslavia. Furthermore, it had no military force at its disposal and no experience in organizing one so that the deployment of troops for peacekeeping, fact-finding or deterrent purposes was not an option even if decisions had been possible. Similarly, it lacked the authority to impose sanctions. The CSCE was immobilized and dependent on other organizations to take action.

The European Community, "supported by the CSCE," was able to act fairly promptly in an effort to end the fighting in Croatia and in a futile attempt to assist the Yugoslav states to find a new federal structure that would be satisfactory to all the parties. It sought to mediate through the good offices of a special representative and to contain hostilities through the dispatch of unarmed civilian monitors. It provided experienced and skillful negotiators. But the EC quickly encountered problems that seriously handicapped its efforts. First, it was not accepted by the Yugoslav parties as an impartial third party since various EC members were suspected of favoring either Croatia or Serbia. Germany publicly pushed for recognition of Croatia (and Slovenia) as independent states, which the Serbs viewed as a hostile attitude.

Second, the EC, like the CSCE, did not have the capacity to field a peace-keeping force as a means of stabilizing the situation. The unarmed observers, whose only protection was distinctive white uniforms, were ineffective.

The Western European Union (WEU), a largely dormant Western European military organization, was activated to organize a peace-keeping operation, but this failed partly because there were no readily available troops, partly because there was no command and control machinery in place, but mostly because the organization was unable to agree on the purpose for which a force would be deployed. Neither the EC nor the WEU has a central executive comparable to the Secretary-General of the United Nations capable of managing a peace-keeping operation.

As a regional organization NATO has been effective in the maintenance of security in Europe through military deterrence. It is essentially a defense organization, although its Charter (Article 2) encourages economic cooperation among members. It has no specific mandate for conflict resolution. The disintegration of the Warsaw Pact and of the Soviet Union inevitably affected NATO's orientation and caused a search for new missions. Peacekeeping emerged as one of these. When the conflict in Yugoslavia broke out, it was generally considered unthinkable that NATO could play a role in bringing it under control. While it had adequate, well-trained and well-equipped troops, it was widely assumed that it had no mandate to use them outside the NATO area, as Yugoslavia clearly was. NATO's responsibility was to deal with threats to its members from *other states*, not to restore peace *within* nonmember states. The NATO Secretary-General, Manfred Woerner, had stated in a 1991 interview that the organization should be "the focal point of a new pan-European security structure" and that as an expanded defense community it would eventually put peace-keeping forces in places of ethnic or border unrest "from the Atlantic ocean to the Ural mountains."[10] But Woerner added that he was expressing his personal opinion since consensus had proven elusive.

The fact that within two years NATO had begun to assist in the enforcement of a UN arms embargo against the Yugoslav states, well outside NATO territory, that it had offered to provide peace-keeping forces for the CSCE, and was poised to send war planes against the Bosnian Serbs in behalf of the United Nations is indicative of how quickly attitudes have changed in the post–Cold War period and how forcefully events in Yugoslavia have influenced thinking regarding international security in Europe. NATO has now tentatively indicated a willingness to act as the peace-keeping arm of the CSCE and it has begun joint peace-keeping exercises with countries in Eastern Europe that have joined with NATO in the Partnership for Peace.

Yet, there are circumstances that can make the wide utilization of NATO troops in resolving regional conflicts problematic. NATO, like the CSCE, acts on the basis of consensus and there are evident differences within the organization on who is to exercise command and control of NATO troops if they are deployed at the behest of another organization, either the UN or the CSCE. Moreover, German troops, one of the largest NATO contingents, may take part in military operations outside the NATO area under the auspices of the United Nations only if they are approved by the Bundestag in principle prior to deployment.[11] (Germany has shared in enforcing the sanctions against Yugoslavia and sent troops to Somalia to participate in UNOSOM II but these were interpreted as non-combat missions.)

Neither NATO nor the WEU has any presence, not even liaison offices, at the UN nor is there any formal agreement between either the CSCE or the European Community defining their relationship with the UN. This was a distinct disadvantage when NATO agreed to undertake military enforcement action in behalf of the UN in Bosnia. Rules of engagement were agreed to only after different and sometimes acrimonious negotiations.

In summary, the European institutions, when faced with the Yugoslav situation (which may well be replicated elsewhere) were hampered in decision-making because of the consensus requirement in the CSCE and NATO. Neither the CSCE nor the EC has a peace-keeping or peace-enforcement capacity unless NATO becomes available for this purpose. The extent to which NATO will meet this need is still unclear despite the favorable position taken by the NATO Council. Neither NATO nor the WEU is willing to be bound by a decision of the Security Council. Moreover, the authority of the EC to apply sanctions does not extend beyond its members, which makes an embargo hardly effective. (A regional organization is, in any event, not authorized to take enforcement action under Chapter VII of the UN Charter unless it has been asked to do so by the Security Council although, as mentioned, the EC called on its members to impose sanctions against Yugoslavia.)

THE UN ADVANTAGE

What, then, can be concluded concerning the role of the United Nations in dealing with regional threats to security? What effective action can the UN take that regional organizations cannot? What can the UN do to support the efforts of the regional organizations in seeking to control and resolve intrastate conflict? Again an examination of the UN role in Yugoslavia provides some answers to these questions.

The UN action in response to the Yugoslav conflict can be summarized as follows:

1. "Concerned that continuation of the situation constitutes a threat to international peace and security,"[12] the Security Council expressed full support for the European efforts, thus adding an authority that the Europeans felt would be useful.

2. In response to the request of the parties, who did not trust the objectivity of the EC, the Security Council invited the Secretary-General to offer his assistance in consultation with the Government of Yugoslavia and the European organizations to bring an end to hostilities in Yugoslavia.

3. Acting under Chapter VII of the Charter, the Council embargoed the shipment of weapons and military equipment to Yugoslavia and imposed comprehensive sanctions against Serbia and Montenegro.

4. A Personal Envoy, appointed by the Secretary-General as a UN representative, mediated a cease-fire in Croatia.

5. The UN joined with the EC in an effort to mediate a Bosnian settlement.

6. The Security Council authorized first the deployment of a military observer mission and then a full-scale peace-keeping force to

> maintain the cease-fire agreement in Croatia achieved through UN mediation.
>
> 7. The UN established a symbolic peace-keeping presence in Sarajevo in the hope of preventing the outbreak of conflict there. It then deployed a limited peace-keeping force to secure the airport for humanitarian deliveries and, with subsequent expansion, to provide security for the delivery of humanitarian assistance where needed in the country, resorting ultimately to enforcement measures under Chapter VII of the UN Charter to implement this mandate and to afford protection to designated safe areas.
>
> 8. The UN carried out a major humanitarian relief program under the leadership of the UN High Commissioner for Refugees.
>
> 9. The Security Council established a War Crimes Tribunal for Yugoslavia and a committee to identify the persons to be tried.
>
> 10. The UN deployed a modest *deterrent* peace-keeping force in Macedonia at the request of the Macedonian Government but without the consent of neighboring Serbia, the party being deterred.

The UN action, like that of the EC, has been subject to wide criticism as being ineffective. It is not yet clear whether the application of the UN measures, in conjunction with the mediation efforts of the European Community, will be sufficient to bring peace to the various states that comprised Yugoslavia, or whether it will be a satisfactory peace. They could not prevent the long continuation of the war in Bosnia. Still, it is clear that the UN had a far greater capacity than the regional organizations to act in this regional struggle. Specifically, the UN provided the following key elements that the regional organizations could not:

- the recognized impartiality required for successful mediation;
- the capacity to deploy a large peace-keeping force under adequate, if imperfect, command and control;
- the authority to impose sanctions that are mandatory on all UN member states;
- the ability to mobilize global support for humanitarian assistance and to provide the machinery and leadership for a massive humanitarian program.
- the capacity to take enforcement action under Chapter VII of the Charter for the protection of humanitarian services and peace-keeping personnel and, in limited measure, to civilian victims of the conflict.

The Yugoslav experience tested the capacity of the UN, as well as of regional organizations, to deal with regional conflicts. The conflicts that erupted in Croatia and subsequently in Bosnia were essentially intrastate in nature although they had obvious international implications. The actions taken by the United Nations, for the most part by decision of the Security Council, were significant as constituting a new interpretation of Article 2, paragraph 7. of the UN Charter prohibiting intervention in domestic affairs of states. The Canadian Secretary of State for External Affairs spoke to this matter in the following terms: "The concept of sovereignty is, of course, fundamental to statehood. . . . But the concept of sovereignty must respect higher principles. The time has now passed when the wanton destruction of human life is a matter of purely internal consideration."[13] The Yugoslav Permanent Representative told the Security Council that the Yugoslav example "might identify the new concept of the United Nations."[14] One cannot yet assume that this concept will be applicable in all circumstances. Only a week later the Council was unable to adopt a resolution regarding the military coup in Haiti with its attendant loss of life because of concern on the part of some members that this would constitute interference in Haiti's internal affairs. The Security Council did not intervene with military force until very late to halt the wanton destruction of human life in Bosnia, and then only hesitantly. Nonetheless, the Yugoslav experience demonstrated that the UN can take action in internal conflict situations, a reality that was to be even more clearly demonstrated in Somalia.

The Macedonian request for the deployment of a UN peace-keeping force in order to *deter* a possible Serbian attack also tested a previously established limit on UN action. As noted in an earlier chapter, Secretary-General Boutros-Ghali had recommended in *An Agenda for Peace* that the possibility of the deterrent deployment of peacekeepers with the consent of only one party to a conflict be considered. The Security Council had not responded to this recommendation at the time of the Macedonian request. It nonetheless acted favorably on the Secretary-General's proposal that a deterrent force be sent to Macedonia. Thus the admissibility of this action was established by action rather than by a decision on principle. The action gave reassurance to Macedonia and may have prevented a Serbian intrusion.

The major weakness in the UN's efforts in Yugoslavia was its inability, within the limitations of the peace-keeping concept, to force the parties to comply with cease-fire agreements they reached or to establish the degree of security needed for the safe delivery of humanitarian assistance to elements in need. It could provide only limited protection to the civilian population.

The performances of regional organizations and the UN in post–Cold War conflicts in other areas have been similar to those evident in Yugoslavia, although sometimes with greater success. In Central America peacekeeping could only be done by the United Nations, albeit with participation of troops from the region. Mediation responsibilities were shared by the UN and OAS except in El Salvador where the UN acted alone. In Somalia the UN provided the required peace-keeping and peace-enforcement operations (in part by authorizing the United States to lead a military action in its behalf) and was the principal mediator, in cooperation with the League of Arab States, the Organization of African Unity, and the Organization of the Islamic Conference in seeking an end to the fighting and national reconciliation. What is striking is the inability of the regional organizations, acting alone, to handle conflicts in their region. The capacity to impose effective sanctions is limited as shown by the experience of the EC in Yugoslavia and of the OAS in Haiti where countries outside the hemisphere did not comply. Their ability to undertake peace-keeping operations is severely limited either by a lack of resources as in the OAU, a lack of deployable troops as in the EC, or a lack of common will as in the OAS. Their objectivity tends to be suspect in the eyes of parties to conflicts who, for this reason, prefer to have UN involvement in mediation efforts. This is unfortunate at a time when the UN is overburdened and possibly overextended and is itself handicapped by a continuing insufficiency of funds.

Secretary-General Boutros-Ghali suggested in *An Agenda for Peace* that regional organizations possess a potential that should be utilized in preventive diplomacy, peacekeeping, peacemaking and postconflict peace-building. While the Security Council has the primary responsibility for maintaining international security, regional action could, he states, "not only lighten the burden of the Council but also contribute to a deeper sense of participation, consensus and democratization." The Security Council, in turn, in January 1993, invited regional organizations to study, on a priority basis, "ways and means to strengthen their functions to maintain international peace and security within their areas of competence." The Council suggested that they might consider, in particular, "preventive diplomacy including fact-finding, confidence-building, good offices, peace-building, and, where appropriate, peacekeeping."[15]

The present potential of the regional organizations in these fields varies greatly. Confidence-building measures have been an important part of CSCE objectives since its inception. It has introduced programs for mutual observation of military maneuvers and the exchange of visits by senior military officers and other similar measures. Through its human rights watch it promotes a transparency among its members that also contributes to confidence building. Alone among the regional organizations it has established a Conflict Reduction Center that, until now, has been largely concerned with the realization of the military confidence-building measures agreed on on by CSCE members. Its staff is minimal and its present responsibilities are narrowly defined. Nonetheless, it could be developed into a useful instrument for fact-finding, data collection, information exchange and treaty monitoring, including arms control agreements. If its potential is realized, it could serve as a model for similar centers in other regional organizations.

The CSCE, depending on the availability of NATO forces, also has the potential capacity to undertake peace-keeping operations in Europe. Given the large and disparate membership of CSCE and the consensus basis of decisions, agreement to embark on a peace-keeping or peace enforcement mission may prove difficult to reach. Moreover, The CSCE has no command and control capacity and no executive head competent to manage a peace-keeping operation. The command and control function could, however, be exercised by NATO in CSCE-authorized deployments. The two organizations could together develop contingency plans for peace-keeping operations. Adequate financial and manpower resources are obviously available within the CSCE community to support peacekeeping.

The European Union, being smaller and with greater homogeneity, is better able to make decisions than the CSCE. In the case of Yugoslavia it assumed a security responsibility beyond its geographic extent. This is not, however, a mandated responsibility. In the new states that were formerly part of the Soviet Union the CSCE has assumed observer functions (along with the UN) rather than the EC. It is, thus, not clear whether the European Community (formerly the EC) will be permanently active in the security field or if it will step in only when the CSCE is unable to take action. The WEU is participating, along with NATO, in maintaining the UN embargo on trade with Serbia and Montenegro. In theory it could provide peace-keeping forces for utilization in European Union-authorized programs. This was not successful in Yugoslavia. Strengthening of the EU's peace-keeping potential will require substantial enhancement of the WEU's military capability and the development of some kind of central command and control authority for such operations. Notwithstanding its decision-making problems, the CSCE would seem, in the longer term, to be the more appropriate regional security instrumentality with the EU serving to complement its efforts.

NATO is engaged in extensive confidence-building measures with Russia and other members of the former Warsaw Pact that should be effective in increasing military transparency in Europe. As an organization it had had no experience in peacekeeping, peace-enforcement or fact-finding prior to its until now very limited involvement in the conflict in Yugoslavia. However, it is well equipped to carry out such operations either in behalf of the CSCE or the United Nations provided satisfactory command arrangements can be worked out.

In sum, the several regional organizations in Europe, when seen together, offer substantial future potential for the maintenance of security in Europe and for relieving the United Nations in the future of burdens originating on that continent. The disappointing performance of the CSCE and the EC in Yugoslavia should not be seen as necessarily defining their future possibilities.

The OAS, as has been described earlier, has had some success as a mediator of hemispheric disputes and in the limited deployment of peace-keeping forces. A number of South American countries have provided troop contingents to the UN for peacekeeping—mostly for early peace-keeping undertakings but recently in Central America and Cambodia. Canada's recent accession means that the OAS now includes one of the most experienced countries in peacekeeping. A staff college for training hemispheric officers exists and could provide appropriate training. Unlike Europe, however, no machinery is in place in the OAS for early warning and conflict prevention and only limited confidence-building measures have been undertaken, and those mostly on a bilateral basis. The OAS has long had the image of an organization in decline. The enhancement of its peace-keeping capacity, together with the establishment of machinery for information exchange and fact-finding, could serve not only the interests of security in the hemisphere but also contribute to the revitalization of the organization. While the dominant—sometimes domineering—position of the United States poses special problems for collective action on the part of the OAS, the potential is there for the OAS to play a more effective security role in the future.

It is not possible to be as optimistic about the Organization of African Unity. As noted earlier, it has established a Mechanism for Conflict Prevention, Management and Resolution that offers promise. Underlying this initiative was the conviction that African states should be responsible for the security of their continent. However, the OAU lacks access to adequate resources, is frequently divided, and has not, until now, been notably successful in building confidence among members. It did not find it possible to prevent the conflicts in Somalia or Rwanda. It has no information gathering capacity. All in all, the potential of the OAU to contribute to the security of the African continent remains quite limited. It will need a great deal of help in responding to the Security Council's invitation to strengthen its functions.

The potential of the League of Arab States for the maintenance of peace in the region is similarly limited, albeit for different reasons. Adequate financial and military resources are available but the requisite political agreement among its members for collective action is lacking. Confidence-building is urgently needed that will only be possible in conjunction with a harmonization of interests and ambitions among League members. The Arab-Israeli relationship, while improving, obviously prejudices the possibility for any Arab organization to exercise principal responsibility for the resolution of disputes and the maintenance of peace in the region.

ASEAN is not organized to deal with military aspects of security. It is not realistic to think of the enhancement of its peacekeeping capability since none exists. On the other hand it clearly is concerned with enhancing security in the Pacific area. It has done much to increase confidence among its members through frequent consultation and harmonization of policies. Now ASEAN is reaching out to non-member Pacific states such as Japan and the Republic of Korea to bring them within the framework of the organization's nonmilitary confidence-building measures. While ASEAN cannot be expected to share any burdens of peacekeeping and peace-enforcement in Southeast Asia, it is reasonable to expect that its contribution to confidence-building, peacemaking and fact-finding can be enhanced.

In reviewing the possibilities for strengthening regional organizations for the purposes of maintaining international security, one must face, at this point, an unhappy reality: There are two extremely sensitive regions where no regional arrangements exist—South Asia and the Northern Pacific. In South Asia the development of a regional security organization that would include India and Pakistan is unlikely. In North Asia, UN Secretaries-General Waldheim and Pérez de Cuéllar repeatedly offered their good offices to bring about a reduction of tension on the Korean peninsula and facilitate communication between the North and the South. The offers were not accepted. Secretary-General Boutros-Ghali has also visited Korea, hoping, in particular, to bring North Korean compliance with the terms of the Nuclear Non-Proliferation Treaty. While communication between the two parts of Korea has improved, the situation remains dangerous. In some ways the situation in the Northern Pacific is analogous to that in Europe at the time the CSCE was formed. The countries of the region are ideologically divided but aware of a growing mutuality of interests, including (except for the North Koreans) restraint on North Korean nuclear intentions. The concept of a North Pacific conference for security and cooperation is not new, but with Cold War rivalries over, it has become a more realistic possibility. Even if one is formed, however, it would likely have the same strengths and weaknesses as the CSCE in maintaining regional security. It might well be successful in organizing confidence-building measures, in encouraging respect for human rights and possibly in the peaceful resolution of disputes. However, a peace-keeping or peace-enforcement capability would lie far in the future, if then.

THE POTENTIAL FOR GREATER COOPERATION
BETWEEN THE UN AND REGIONAL ORGANIZATIONS

In *An Agenda for Peace* Secretary-General Boutros-Ghali suggested that the design of cooperative work between regional organizations and the UN must adapt to the realities of each case with flexibility and creativity. As has been shown, the present capabilities and future potential of the various organizations vary greatly. In every case, however, a good bit can be gained from closer working contact between the organizations and the UN and from the development of a network among them for a continuing exchange of information and mutual support.

Peacekeeping and preventive diplomacy are two fields related to international security in which enhanced and structured cooperation between the UN and regional organizations, *mutatis mutandi*, can be especially productive. The United Nations has amassed much valuable experience in peacekeeping and in such elements of peace-building as election monitoring, institution building, and the assurance of respect for human rights. By sharing this experience through training programs, the United Nations can hasten the day when regional organizations can assume a greater share of the burden and do so effectively. Peacekeeping training afforded by the United Nations could cover not only the preparation of national troops for participation in UN peace-keeping or peace-enforcement operations, but also the preparation of regional organizations to undertake peace-keeping operations themselves. The European organizations and the OAS are at a stage where they could profit from such assistance now. The UN could profit, in reverse, from assistance from NATO in strengthening its command and control capacity. Consultations of a purely exploratory nature could be initiated with the OAU and the League of Arab States while recognizing that their peace-keeping potential is likely to remain limited for a good time to come.

A great deal of information should be readily available to a regional organization concerning potentially destabilizing developments in the area. Information needs to be analyzed in both the regional and global context if those responsible for early warning at the UN and at the regional level are to understand fully its import and reach conclusions on counteractions that can be taken. Clearly the early warning capability of the UN would be strengthened if information relative to international security available at the local level were collected by regional organizations and would become the subject of regular consultation with the office or offices in the UN responsible for preventive diplomacy and peacemaking. Another benefit of such a practice, if carried out by a regional organization, would be the encouragement of greater transparency within the region and greater confidence among the regional states—unless the intentions of one or more of them are shown to be less than pacific.

None of the regional organizations has, at this time, a unit responsible for the collection and analysis of information relevant to security. The CSCE Conflict Prevention Centre should be capable of undertaking this function and the OAU Mechanism for Conflict Prevention is well suited, at least by purpose, to do this work in Africa. The UN, itself, no longer has a unit specifically designed for data collection and analysis. The UN Secretary-General could take two actions that would encourage the development of a "security information network." The first action would be to designate an office in the Secretariat as the center for contact and exchange with regional organizations. The second action would be to organize consultations among these organizations and the UN to explore together 1) what information is needed, 2) what sources can be exploited, 3) what kind of mutually compatible information and analysis units should be established at the regional level, and 4) how the network should function for the sustained benefit of all sides.

The CSCE experience has shown that regional organizations are well-suited to introduce various kinds of confidence-building measures. In the UN a number of studies have been completed on confidence-building measures that could be of benefit to those regions other than Europe where little has so far been done. This suggests the value of a broader consultative process that could bring representatives of the various regional organizations, initially, at least, under the aegis of the UN, to exchange experiences, review needs and consider how one grouping might be of assistance to another. Through such a process a connecting, supportive network could develop, complementary to a security information exchange network, that would facilitate the growth of confidence-building measures, lending to them, as appropriate, the auspices of the UN. In some regions, such as the Persian Gulf, the United Nations might be best suited to take the initiative, taking advantage of the advice of the regional organizations concerned. This procedure would have the additional benefit of nurturing a deeper sense of democratic participation by regional organizations in the maintenance of global peace.

The poor performance of regional organizations in preventing conflict, especially in the former Yugoslavia, Somalia and Rwanda has deflated a good many hopes that they could soon relieve the UN of some part of its burden. Certainly there should now be no illusions. Only the CIS and NATO have an effective peace-keeping capability and both entail special problems if they operate separately from the UN. None has experience or a functioning structure for conflict prevention. This should not mean that the goal of enhanced cooperation between the regional organizations and the UN is invalid. There is a realistic prospect that, in time, the European organizations and the OAS can undertake independent peace-keeping operations without encumbering UN resources. All of the organizations have some prospect, with the assistance of the UN, in confidence building (including regional arms limitation planning) and in conflict prevention. The UN will become a stronger force for peace if it persists in efforts for a more productive relationship with the regional groupings and for improved effectiveness on their parts even if the results are some time in coming.

NOTES

1. Speech in The Hague, May 7, 1948. Cited in Inis Claude, *Swords into Plowshares* (New York: Random House, 1984), p. 113.

2. Edward R. Stettinius, Jr., *Report to the President on the Results of the San Francisco Conference* (Department of State, June 26, 1945), p. 109.

3. The North Atlantic Treaty, Preamble and Articles 1,5,7.

4. UN Document S/RES/836, 1993.

5. Declaration of Heads of State and Government, 29th Ordinary Session, 28–30 June 1993. OAU Document AHG/Decl. 3 (XXIX), Rev. 1.

6. Statement of the Secretary-General of the OAU, Dr. Salim Ahmed Salim, to the inaugural meeting of the Control Organ at OAU Headquarters, 13 September 1993, in OAU press release of that date.

7. Andre Kozyrev, "The Lagging Partnership," *Foreign Affairs*, May–June, 1994, p. 68.

8. Distributed at the UN as General Assembly Document A/45/859, 12 December 1990.

9. "Statements and Speeches." German Information Center (New York) Press Release, June 19, 1991, pp. 1–2.

10. *Washington Post*, 4 October 1991, p. A19.

11. Decision of the German Federal Constitutional Court. German Information Center (New York) Press Release, July 1994.

12. Security Council Resolution 713, 25 September 1991.

13. Security Council Document S/23076, 25 September 1991.

14. UN Press Release SC/5309, 25 September 1991.

15. Note by the President of the Security Council, Document S/25184, 29 January 1993.

8

The Secretary-General as Chief Administrative Officer of a United Nations Under Challenge

The greatly increased international security activities of the United Nations that began in 1987 and have grown ever since have placed an unprecedented burden on the staff and structure of the organization, beginning inevitably with the Secretary-General. The first Secretary-General described the job as the most difficult in the world. It has become even more demanding as the responsibilities of the United Nations for peacekeeping and peacemaking, for resolving conflict and providing humanitarian assistance, have grown exponentially without equivalent growth (or improvement) in the resources on which the Secretary-General can call. The former U.S. Attorney-General, Dick Thornburgh, in a report submitted to the Secretary-General in March 1993 on relinquishing the post of Under-Secretary-General for Administration and Management in the Secretariat, stated that the United Nations Organization "today truly stands at a crossroads as to whether or not it can effectively adapt to these changing times. . . . The new responsibilities being assumed by the United Nations have raised the stakes and heightened the consequences in terms of human suffering should the United Nations fail to accomplish [its] new goals."[1]

The position of the Secretary-General is somewhat analogous to that of chief executive officer of a transnational corporation. The principal undertakings of "UN Inc." relate to peace, economic and social development and the various aspects of human security. Its board of directors is composed of most of the governments of the world, a few of whom own the majority of the stock and are therefore more influential than the others. The position of Secretary-General is described in the United Nations Charter as that of chief administrative officer and not much more is said about it. Yet the managerial and diplomatic skills, the political acumen and the talent for persuasion of this individual can influence substantially the success or failure of the United Nations in meeting the new and expanded tasks that have been described in the preceding chapters.

As a specially designated group in the Department of State was developing plans during World War II for a new international organization that would become the United Nations the importance of the administrative function of its executive head (then usually referred to as "General Secretary" or "Director-General" and sometimes even as "President") was recognized. Not much attention was given to defining it, however, since it was assumed that administration of the new organization would follow the pattern already set in the League of Nations. Primary attention was given instead to the addition of a political dimension to the position. There was even the thought of having the "Director-General" chair the meetings of the Security Council. In the end the political function was encapsulated primarily in Article 99 which authorizes the Secretary-General to bring to the attention of the Security Council any development that, in his opinion, may threaten the maintenance of international peace and security. Most of the other tasks assigned to him inevitably entail a political dimension, even the formulation of the UN budget.

Since the Secretary-General, under the Charter, acts as chief administrative officer "in all meetings of the General Assembly, of the Security Council, and of the Trusteeship Council, and shall perform such other functions as are entrusted to him by these organs" his responsibilities extend to the economic and social activities of the United Nations as well as the political. The Secretary-General must be concerned with the entire agenda of the United Nations from human rights to the environment, from peacemaking to humanitarian assistance programs, from disarmament to the illegal trafficking in drugs. The utilization in the Charter of the term "chief administrative officer" to describe the functions of the Secretary-General is, if taken literally, misleading. His responsibilities can be best understood as falling under two headings: managerial and substantive. The two are in competition for his time and attention with the substantive almost always winning.

The wisdom of combining potentially expansive political functions with responsibility for the administration of the organization was questioned on grounds of efficiency even as the plans for the United Nations were still at an early stage of development. But it was expected that the administrative aspects of the position, which were considered less important, could be "delegated,"[2] leaving the head of the Secretariat free to concentrate primarily on his political and other substantive functions. This thinking continued through the Dumbarton Oaks and the San Francisco Conferences. On neither occasion was any particular attention given to defining what the administrative responsibilities of the Secretary-General would be or how they should be performed. This is partly accounted for (besides by the League precedent) by the expectation that there would be four or five deputy secretaries-general, elected in the same manner as the Secretary-General, with the authority that election would convey. One elected deputy would have been responsible for administration. This idea was rejected in the end, notwithstanding the strong support of the Soviet Union, on the ground that it would compromise the independence of the Secretariat if the deputies to the Secretary-General were dependent on the votes of governments for their positions. So there has never been a deputy secretary-general with full authority to manage the organization. Moreover, the United Nations, as an administrative structure, developed into a very different animal from the League of Nations, so that what had worked there did not provide an adequate guide for UN procedures or management.

ASSESSING A SECRETARY-GENERAL'S PERFORMANCE

A number of states have been highly critical of political actions taken by a Secretary-General. The Soviet Union, for example, sharply attacked the actions of Trygve Lie in connection with the Korean war and of Dag Hammarskjöld on the Congo crisis. A number of Western countries were also unhappy in connection with the latter case and over the withdrawal by U Thant of the United Nations Emergency Peace-keeping Force (UNEF) from the Sinai in 1967. Indeed, the Soviet Union refused in the Security Council to concur in recommending the election of Trygve Lie for a second term and it withdrew recognition of Dag Hammarskjöld as Secretary-General, motivated in both cases by dissatisfaction with "political" actions. But for the past twenty years the Secretary-General has for the most part been commended for his political actions. When there has been criticism in the political field it has often been for administrative weaknesses that have jeopardized political effectiveness, hardly ever for political judgement or lack thereof or for inadequacy as a mediator.

There have been repeated calls for more effective preventive diplomacy. But here, too, emphasis has been on strengthening the administrative structure to provide the support needed for early warning and a global watch to make preventive diplomacy more feasible. Only with the recent advent of the extremely difficult questions regarding the use by the UN of military force in internal crises and the election of an outspoken, strong-willed Secretary-General has criticism again been voiced concerning the political—or political/military—judgment of the Secretary-General. There have been, at the same time, some calls to increase his authority so that he might better deal with post–Cold War security emergencies.

The situation has been comparable in the other areas of the Secretary-General's substantive competence as well. The United Nations has been subjected to almost constant criticism from member states for inadequate leadership in economic affairs and, until recently at least, in such an important social field as human rights. But the criticism has seldom been directed at the Secretary-General except, again, for administrative weakness in failing to produce an effective organizational structure and ensure adequate coordination within the UN system. It is perhaps in part a matter of expectations. No government really expects a John Maynard Keynes as Secretary-General, even though, if one excludes the large amounts now required for peacekeeping, some ninety percent of the UN's resources are devoted to economic and social programs. It may also stem from a wide and resigned realization that no Secretary-General can do much to improve the economic and social structure of the UN system, since change depends on the governments themselves and, until recently, they have found neither the will nor the consensus to bring real improvement.

THE IMPACT OF POST–COLD WAR RELATIONS

The political functions of the Secretary-General have been highlighted by the new activism of the Security Council more than other substantive areas of his responsibility. This has direct implications for his managerial function. As the demands on the UN for peacekeeping, peace-building, humanitarian assistance and other activities of high political sensitivity have escalated in the post–Cold War years, the management aspects of the position have become more demanding and more politically charged. To cite an illustrative example: As noted in an earlier chapter, the General Assembly and the Security Council have both called for an enhancement of the UN's preventive diplomacy and early warning capacity. The majority of members insist at the same time on a no-growth budget. In his administrative capacity, the Secretary-General must somehow find the necessary resources, or risk failure on the part of the UN to carry out these preventive functions in the present, more promising international atmosphere where failure can no longer be attributed to the effects of the Cold War. Governments clearly think that a Secretary-General should have the management skills of an outstanding corporate executive along with the political ability on which the effectiveness of the UN in the maintenance of international security so heavily depends. They have not found the management skills present in adequate measure in any of the secretaries-general until now.

PERENNIAL POOR MARKS FOR UN ADMINISTRATION

Criticism of the administration of the UN is not a recent phenomenon. As set forth in innumerable internal and external reports it has been sustained and unvarnished. The "Group of High Level Intergovernmental Experts" appointed to review the efficiency of the administrative and financial functioning of the United Nations in 1986, before the thaw in the Cold War was evident, concluded that "management capacity, especially with regard to the need to maintain overall administrative efficiency, productivity and cost effectiveness, has lagged behind [the] pace of growth. The quality of work needs to be improved upon. The qualifications of staff, in particular in the higher categories, are inadequate and the working methods are not efficient. Today's structure is too complex, fragmented and top-heavy."[3] Secretary-General Boutros-Ghali, when he assumed office in 1992, sought to overcome the problem of top-heaviness by eliminating some twenty-five percent of the most senior positions and a number of departments and offices in the Secretariat (without, however, reducing the number of lower-ranking staff). Nonetheless, in the report referred to earlier, Dick Thornburgh, the outgoing Under-Secretary-General for Administration and Management, stated that "many of the administrative and management practices of the past 45 years are wholly inadequate to meet the demands of the current era. If initiatives to change and modernize these practices are not forthcoming, this Organization simply will not have the ability to meet its new responsibilities."[4]

THE SECRETARY-GENERAL'S STAFF

In the many discussions that take place on the desirable qualifications for the Secretary-General, management ability is almost always placed high on the list. Precisely because the criticism and calls for improvement are so widespread it may be useful to examine in pragmatic terms the conditions under which the Secretary-General functions in the substantive and administrative management of the organization.

The Preparatory Commission of the United Nations, having much in mind the League pattern, developed a structure for the Secretariat that consisted of eight departments, each headed by an assistant-secretary-general.

- Security Council Affairs
- Economic Affairs
- Social Affairs
- Trusteeship and Non-Self-Governing Territories
- Public Information

- Legal Counsel
- Administrative and Financial Services
- Conference and General Services

In approving this plan, the General Assembly authorized the Secretary-General to "make such changes in the initial structure as may be required to the end that the most effective distribution of responsibilities and functions among the units of the Secretariat may be achieved."[5] Taking advantage of this authorization, each Secretary-General (and member states as well) has, in fact, sought to achieve a more effective distribution of responsibilities and functions. Economic and social matters have been organized by Secretary-General Boutros-Ghali into three departments rather than two (after having previously consolidated them into one) and the Security Council, General Assembly and Trusteeship departments have been consolidated into a Department of Political Affairs. A Department of Peacekeeping Affairs has been added. But to an extent that is surprising in light of the growth in size and responsibilities of the United Nations, the structure devised by the Preparatory Commission for the Secretariat has remained fundamentally intact. The boxes on the charts have only been rearranged or renamed. Were he to come back today, Trygve Lie would recognize the central elements of the Secretariat as he organized it. The major changes have been in the size—from a Secretariat staff of 2,450 to one of just over 10,000—and in the addition of numerous functional offices and programs spread widely over the world concerned with economic and social problems.

Thus, in addition to New York, there are three "headquarters" cities, Geneva, Vienna and Nairobi, each of which is the location of functional offices such as the Office of the High Commissioner for Refugees (Geneva), the UN Environmental Program (Nairobi) and various offices related to the control of narcotic drugs (Vienna). There are also five regional economic commissions located in Santiago, Geneva, Addis Ababa, Bangkok and Amman.[6] All of these organizations, like the UN Development Program (UNDP), the Fund for Population Activities and UNICEF in New York, fall in principle within the managerial responsibility of the Secretary-General. However, those that are supported largely by voluntary contributions and have their own governing boards—for example, UNICEF, UNDP and the High Commissioner for Refugees—are largely independent and responsible for their own administration and policies. In Bosnia, where the High Commissioner for Refugees was given overall responsibility for humanitarian assistance, the High Commissioner, on at least one occasion, decided to withdraw personnel from areas under Bosnian Serb attack without consulting the Secretary-General and, it turned out, quite contrary to his views on what should be done.

The Secretary-General is dependent on this structure for the implementation of the substantive policies for which he (or she) is held generally responsible by member states, as well as for the management of the organization. He is dependent on the various offices, over some of which he has little control, for both substantive and managerial support. This includes the servicing of the many intergovernmental organs and bodies of the UN for which the Secretary-General, as Chief Administrative Officer, is also responsible.

In summary, the main elements of the UN bureaucratic structure on which the Secretary-General must depend are

- A Secretariat staff of some 10,000 employees widely dispersed around the world.

- Eight departments in the Secretariat (at the latest count), headed by under-secretaries-general.

- A covey of senior advisors, special representatives, speech writers and protocol functionaries in his immediate office, a growth area under Boutros-Ghali.

- A sizeable number of separate functional and substantive support offices dealing with economic and social matters over some of which the Secretary-General exercises only tenuous authority.[7]

LIMITATIONS ON THE SECRETARY-GENERAL'S FREEDOM OF ACTION

In his definitive lecture "The International Civil Servant in Law and in Fact,"[8] Dag Hammarskjöld noted that in Article 97 of the Charter the Secretary-General is described as the "chief administrative officer of the organization," a phrase not found in the Covenant of the League of Nations. "Its explicit inclusion in the Charter," he stated, "made it a constitutional requirement—not simply a matter left to the discretion of the organs—that the administration of the Organization shall be left to the Secretary-General." This has been the wish of each Secretary-General to have full administrative control. It is a constitutional provision, however, that neither member states individually nor the General Assembly has always honored. In a lecture in the same Oxford forum some twenty-five years later, Secretary-General Pérez de Cuéllar commented, "It would be a refreshing change if the General Assembly and individual Member States were to exercise more forbearance and give the Secretary-General the flexibility he needs to ensure the smooth and efficient functioning of the Secretariat."[9]

Despite Dag Hammarskjöld's interpretation of the Charter, there are distinct limitations on the power and freedom of action of the Secretary-

General in administering the United Nations organization that few corporate CEOs would accept. This is a factor in the frequent appearance of ineffectiveness in the Secretary-General's management of the Secretariat. It is revealing to examine what these limitations are in areas important to his managerial leadership.

Bureaucratic Structure

As noted earlier, the Secretary-General was authorized by the first session of the General Assembly to make such changes in the original structure of the Secretariat as may be required to achieve the most effective distribution of responsibilities and functions. Thus the Secretary-General *does* have the power to restructure the Secretariat. For example, Secretary-General Waldheim was responsible for establishing the Centre for Social Development in Vienna (mainly to provide occupants for the huge building that the Austrian Government had built there for international agencies). Boutros-Ghali moved most of it back to New York. Pérez de Cuéllar established the Office for Research and the Collection of Information (ORCI), without reference to the General Assembly. Several member states at first questioned this action because of perceived political implications, but none went so far as to challenge the right of the Secretary-General to take it. However, he was only able to establish the office on the basis of existing resources. All posts and personnel had to be transferred from other offices. No outside recruitment was possible. Any additional expenditure for a new office would require the authorization of the General Assembly.

The Secretary-General cannot on his authority establish new posts if there is no provision for them in the budget as approved by the Assembly. Even to transfer posts from one section of the budget to another requires the approval of the Advisory Committee on Administrative and Budgetary Questions (ACABQ). If the present Secretary-General determines that additional posts are required for an early warning mechanism to meet the challenges of the new era, as the General Assembly has suggested, he must obtain the budgetary authorization of the General Assembly which, illogical as it may seem, has so far not been forthcoming. Before any request for additional resources is made to the Assembly, it is reviewed by the Program Planning Board, a Secretariat body, where the request is assessed in terms of the program budget. When Secretary-General Pérez de Cuéllar wrote personally to the Board recommending that provision be made in the next program budget for additional posts in ORCI to enhance his preventive diplomacy capabilities, the recommendation was rejected. The Secretary-General can overrule the Board, but this means disregarding the advice of an instrumentality established specifically to see to it that program priorities are respected in the allocation of budgetary resources.

Many other examples could be cited that would illustrate the same realities: 1) a Secretary-General can alter the structure of the Secretariat, and this has frequently been done; 2) if additional resources are involved the authorization of the General Assembly is required and this is not always forthcoming; 3) likewise, any move to strengthen an existing program through additional resources requires the approval of the General Assembly; and 4) there are restrictions on the freedom of the Secretary-General to reallocate posts from one section of the budget without the concurrence of the ACABQ.

The Secretary-General, for better or worse, is not the only one who can alter the structure of the Secretariat. The General Assembly, as has been seen, approved the original structure of the Secretariat and it has, ever since, felt free to initiate organizational changes that have directly impacted on the structure of the Secretariat and on the management responsibility of the chief administrative officer. One example: In 1977 the Assembly, acting on the basis of recommendations made by a committee of experts on the economic and social sectors, established the post of Director-General for Development and International Economic Co-operation as the second highest post in the Secretariat. The purpose was to give strong intellectual leadership to the economic programs of the entire UN system, in particular through effective interagency and interdisciplinary coordination. However, as Brian Urquhart and Erskine Childers have pointed out in a Ford Foundation study, the General Assembly left the new Director-General and his office without the authority or the means to fulfill the mandate that the Assembly had established.[10]

This is not to say that the Secretary-General is without influence on such developments. His opinion is always sought. In this particular case Secretary-General Waldheim strongly opposed a proposal that the Director-General should be elected by the General Assembly for fear that the presence of a second elected official in the Secretariat would prejudice his own authority. Secretary-General Boutros-Ghali assumed the power to eliminate the position of Director-General as part of his initial reform effort. His action was not challenged by the General Assembly even though it had created the position.

The Group of High Level Intergovernmental Experts who in 1986 made extensive recommendations for reform of the administration and financial functioning of the United Nations discreetly made their proposals available to the Secretary-General for comment before they were finalized. Indeed, the Group was unable to agree on perhaps the most sensitive question—namely, the size of the recommended cuts in the Secretariat staff—without an indication of what the Secretary-General considered feasible. The chairman of the Group obtained the Secretary-General's view in strict confidence and the figure that the Secretary-General named became the recommendation of the Group.

So the Secretary-General can exert very considerable influence on the decisions of the General Assembly affecting the structure of the Secretariat. The fact remains, however, that the Secretary-General cannot control decisions that can have a very direct bearing on his management of the organization. This problem has assumed greater importance as priorities have shifted in recent years demanding urgent shifts in personnel and resources to peacekeeping and peacemaking.

The Availability of Resources

The power to approve the budget of the United Nations rests entirely with the General Assembly. It also determines how the costs will be apportioned among member states. The responsibility of the Secretary-General is to propose and support, on a biannual basis, a budget that will provide the resources needed for the various programs of the organization. The Secretary-General must manage the United Nations within the financial limits of the approved budget that is almost always less than the one he proposed. A relatively modest contingency fund is included to meet unexpected emergencies. Otherwise, the Secretary-General has little flexibility in increasing resources for programs he may wish to initiate or in transferring resources between programs. As the originator and lobbyist for the biennial budget the Secretary-General can and does have major influence on the appropriation and allocation of resources. But his program proposals are frequently modified by the Assembly and the system imposes severe restraints on his freedom of action as senior manager. This leaves entirely aside the serious problem of the nonpayment of assessed and voluntary contributions by member states that can cripple the Secretary-General's managerial success.

Quality of Staff

Each Secretary-General has insisted on his right to control the formulation and implementation of personnel policy. This has been seen as essential for efficient administration and for the protection of the independence of the international civil service. As a result, personnel is undoubtedly the administrative area in which the Secretary-General has the greatest power. He has supreme authority to appoint, transfer and dismiss staff members of the Secretariat. This is highly important for his ability to manage the organization, for respect of his authority within the Secretariat and for his relations with member states. Yet his control is far from complete.

The wage scales of Secretariat staff members are established by the General Assembly and are not subject to adjustment by the Secretary-General. So, too, are important aspects of the retirement system. If employees demand higher wages or benefits, it is up to the Assembly to grant or deny them. In 1978 the General Assembly resolved that by 1982 twenty-five percent of all professional posts in the Secretariat subject to geographic distribution should be held by women. In 1980 the Assembly went further, asking the Secretary-General to examine additional measures to advance the attainment of policy directives in this area including the possibility of designating a senior official to coordinate these functions. On another occasion the Assembly resolved that a staff member should on transfer or retirement be replaced by a person of the same nationality if the representation in the Secretariat of his or her country were below the median of the desirable range for that country. In the face of an increasing tendency on the part of the Assembly to "legislate" conditions of recruitment and service in the Secretariat, Secretary-General Waldheim and Secretary-General Pérez de Cuéllar each warned against encroachment by the General Assembly on their authority in this area.

A Secretary-General also faces continuing interference from member states on personnel matters. Almost immediately after the first Secretary-General assumed his post, the Soviet Foreign Minister informed him that the five permanent members of the Security Council had agreed that a Soviet national should be appointed as Assistant-Secretary-General for Political and Security Council Affairs. The American secretary of state subsequently confirmed this, adding that the Big Five had decided to ask that a national of each be appointed as assistant-secretary-general. Trygve Lie comments in his memoirs that "by the terms of the Charter, the Secretary-General has full authority in the disposition of the assistant-secretary-generalships. . . . Strictly speaking, therefore, the Big Five had no right to arrive at any understanding regarding the distribution of offices. . . . This is not to say, however, that it would have been politic of me to resist the great-power accord."[11] So it has remained until the present time. The only difference is that the rank has advanced from assistant-secretary-general to under-secretary-general. The permanent members have frequently insisted not just that one of their nationals be appointed as under-secretary-general but that a particular person be given a specific post. When Boutros-Ghali became Secretary-General he suggested in various statements that he would not be bound by consideration of nationality in the appointment of senior staff. He switched the posts occupied by representatives of the five permanent members—the U.S., for example, was given the top administrative post rather than responsibility for the General Assembly. But all five retained posts at the under-secretary-general level. Moreover, Boutros-Ghali three times accepted the specific American nominee for the crucial post of Under-Secretary-General for Administration and Management, two of whom proved unsatisfactory.

Pressure on personnel appointments is not limited to the five permanent members of the Security Council. Few countries refrain from it. The regional groups can be especially persistent on the ground of achieving equitable senior level representation.

The Secretary-General also faces a number of restrictions on the exercise of his authority in the form of the internal rules and regulations of the Secretariat. For example, all proposed recruitment below the senior director level (D-2) must be reviewed by one of the two appointment and promotion bodies. As part of the review process, the files of all staff members who might be qualified for the position are considered. In addition the status of the national quota of any proposed recruit is considered since, according to personnel guidelines, a person from a country that is overrepresented is not to be hired unless it can be demonstrably shown that no qualified candidate is available from a country that is not overrepresented. Because of these procedures, a Secretary-General may find it impossible to obtain the services of a person whom he considers best qualified to fill a particular post. The Secretary-General legally can overrule the appointment and promotion bodies, but in doing so he would be going against a procedure introduced to ensure fairness in staff management and would be subject to criticism both within and outside the Secretariat for mismanagement. In his 1983 Annual Report to the General Assembly, Pérez de Cuéllar stated, "Very often I find myself caught between the directives of the General Assembly, the interests of the staff and the imperatives of good and efficient administration."[12] Such restrictive practices do not fit easily with an activist leadership of a United Nations under challenge.

COORDINATING THE SYSTEM

It is widely expected that the Secretary-General should coordinate the administrative practices and the substantive programs of the entire UN system, including the specialized agencies. Yet nowhere in the Charter is this listed as one of his functions. As chief administrative officer he has authority over all elements of the UN Organization (the structure of which was described earlier) but not over the system as a whole. As has been indicated, his control over such semiautonomous functional offices as the UN Development Program (UNDP), the UN Children's Fund (UNICEF), and the UN Environment Program (UNEP) is nominal, deriving, to the extent it exists, from the fact that he designates or nominates the head of the office. The UN Specialized Agencies, of which there are sixteen, (for example, the World Health Organization, the World Bank and UNESCO), are completely independent and are not, even in theory, subject to the administrative supervision of the UN Secretary-General. He has no influence on the selection of their executive heads.

Under Article 63 of the Charter, the Economic and Social Council (ECOSOC) is authorized to coordinate the activities of the specialized agencies through consultations and recommendations. The article makes no mention of the Secretary-General. As noted earlier, Article 98 of the Charter provides that the Secretary-General shall perform such functions as the principal organs entrust to him. It can be construed that the Secretary-General, in efforts to coordinate the work of the system, is acting in behalf of ECOSOC. To accomplish this, as Secretary-General Boutros-Ghali vigorously set out to do, he must rely on his status as first among equals in relation to the executive heads of the specialized agencies, his chairmanship of the Administrative Committee on Coordination (ACC) and his powers of persuasion. These are weak tools to achieve the kind of coordination that the system badly needs if their combined resources are to contribute with maximum effectiveness to the tasks of conflict deterrence and peace building that are increasingly viewed as essential UN goals.

To summarize, each Secretary-General faces to a greater or lesser extent the following major administrative handicaps that assume even greater importance as the responsibilities of the UN and the expectations placed on it have expanded:

1. Interference by member states in personnel management, having as one result the placement of unqualified personnel in senior positions.
2. A shortage of resources needed for the regular administrative costs of the organization and of humanitarian and security programs.
3. A general lack of managerial ability and training among a culturally diverse Secretariat staff.
4. Inadequate time and energy (and sometimes inclination) to devote to administration.
5. Insufficient authority to achieve coordination among the functional offices and programs and the specialized agencies of the UN system.

POSSIBLE IMPROVEMENTS

Some of these problems should be subject to correction now that governments are, in general, attributing higher priority to the functioning of the UN. Others are not. The most sensitive question is the adequacy of the authority of the Secretary-General, which we will deal with last.

The problem of interference by member states in personnel management was frequently intensified during the Cold War by the distrust and competition between the United States and the Soviet Union. The United States in the early years of the UN demanded that no American of communist persuasion be allowed to serve in the Secretariat and gained the agreement of Trygve Lie that American job applicants should have an American security clearance before being hired. During the Reagan Administration, the United States, by decision of Congress, withheld a portion of its assessed contribution to the regular UN budget (adding to its mounting arrears) on the ground that the dollar salary payments received by Soviet Secretariat employees were financing Soviet espionage activities in the United States. Travel outside of New York City of Secretariat employees from communist countries was severely restricted, which placed the Secretary-General in confrontation with the U.S. since the action in his view was contrary to provisions of the Headquarters Agreement between the U.S. and the UN.

The communist countries, for their part, refused to accept the concept of a career international civil service and insisted that their nationals serve only on fixed term contracts. They were placed in the Secretariat by their governments with small concern for qualifications. This type of difficulty has largely disappeared. Russian and East European nationals are now recruited on the same basis as candidates from most other states. The United States has lifted most of the travel restrictions that it imposed on Secretariat staff members from communist countries.

Ironically, however, the end of the Cold War has tended to intensify, and make more urgent, the major financial problems that confront the Secretary-General. The greatly expanded utilization of peacekeeping has added enormously to the financial difficulties with which the Secretary-General must contend. Peace-keeping costs have multiplied but the willingness or ability of members to pay has not. Even as the work of the UN has become more important in terms of U.S. interests, Washington has fallen deeper into debt. Since the collapse of the Soviet Union, Russia and the other new states of the former Soviet Union have not been able to meet the Soviet assessment, which was the second largest, thus adding to the persistent financial problem.

So the Secretary-General must manage the increased deployment of peace-keeping and peace-enforcement military and civilian personnel with a greater relative shortage of resources than was the case during the Cold War.

There is no doubt that the United Nations is in need of first-class management; that management capacity has lagged behind the pace of growth and the magnitude of challenge. Management capacity, however, has different dimensions. One is the management skill to run an office, to afford effective supervision to subordinate staff, to keep a tight budget, and so on—in other words, administration in a strict sense. The other dimension is that of *executive leadership* or macromanagement. In considering the role of the Secretary-General this distinction is important. For the "first dimension" of administration a Secretary-General must more than ever rely on his subordinate staff.

The problem of inadequate management skills at the level of heads of departments and offices can be alleviated by more extensive training programs. Such programs have been initiated, encouraged by Boutros-Ghali and largely financed on a voluntary basis by Japan. This should help. However, many of the more important posts are filled by persons recruited at a senior rank who assume managerial responsibility without the possibility of midcareer training. The only solution for this, and it is not likely to be entirely satisfactory, is for the Secretary-General to insist on greater selectivity in choosing occupants for these posts.

It has already been noted that from the very beginning the permanent members of the Security Council have expected to have five of the most senior positions and that, further, they expect to provide the candidates for the jobs. To manage the United Nations effectively, the Secretary-General needs good relations with the permanent members. He needs, moreover, to have their confidence in the Secretariat, a concomitant of which is the presence of their nationals in senior Secretariat positions. Persons appointed with the strong backing of a government can on occasion serve as a useful channel for the Secretary-General to that government in connection with both administrative and substantive responsibilities. However, as Trygve Lie, Pérez de Cuéllar and now Boutros-Ghali have done (with only moderate success), the permanent members can be firmly requested to provide not just one candidate for a position but a list from which the Secretary-General can choose. The Secretary-General must be prepared to resist strong pressure from a permanent member in behalf of a favored candidate if he finds the candidate unsuitable. In addition to insisting on the submission of more than one candidate, the Secretary-General can also insist on the freedom to decide which post is to be filled by each country, something that Boutros-Ghali has successfully done.

Wide geographic representation at the most senior levels is obviously desirable. It is not something that a Secretary-General would wish to resist. It is not easy, however, to identify the right African or Japanese or Latin American to fill a particular post. The Secretary-General, to meet successfully the demands of this aspect of his managerial responsibility, needs the assistance of a kind of international headhunters group. It would be advisable for the Secretary-General, or the Under-Secretary-General for Administration and Management in his behalf, to establish an informal advisory group on whose members he could call in confidence to help find the best qualified person in a particular region who might be available for a senior UN post.

Closely related to the managerial task of obtaining a thoroughly competent senior staff is the responsibility to create a structure that will encourage the staff to make their full contribution to the attainment of the goals of the organization. This means opening as many doors as possible to a sense of participation by a broad range of Secretariat personnel in the substantive work in which the Secretary-General, himself, is engaged. As chief administrative officer, the Secretary-General needs to instill a sense of participation and purpose throughout the staff of the organization he leads.

A compartmentalization that has grown increasingly rigid over the years has worked against this in the United Nations. It has not been alleviated by the seemingly arbitrary changes that Secretary-General Boutros-Ghali has made in the Secretariat. The opportunity for field service in operations such as Namibia, Central America and Cambodia has served to reinvigorate staff members by taking them out of the strict confines of departments or offices and allowing them to work on an important undertaking as part of an interdisciplinary UN team. With the many cross-disciplinary threats to global security a comparable team approach should be encouraged at the major UN centers.

In an era when communication is of paramount importance, the UN has remained notably lacking in communication skills. Much of the burden of explaining to governments and to the world public the necessity of using military force to bring peace and overcome humanitarian crises inevitably falls on the Secretary-General and other UN spokespersons. Similarly, the necessary support of governments for UN programs depends not only on the performance of UN staff members but also on the image that governments have of this performance, which is sometimes quite inaccurate. The Secretary-General must take the lead (developing the communication skills, if necessary) in presenting to the world the validity and the necessity of UN programs for the new era. The Secretary-General must be able to make completely clear what he or she needs—and what is not acceptable—in the interest of maintaining an organization that can support with maximum efficiency the ambitious programs mandated by the Assembly and the Security Council. The Secretary-General must more than ever articulate the substantive objectives in which the whole UN system should be joined and bring leadership and coordination to their pursuit. More will have to be accomplished by persuasion than by power. In this, the new era has brought no change.

A highly important thing that a Secretary-General can do in the interest of his overall leadership of the organization is to appoint as Under-Secretary-General for Administration and Management a person of established managerial ability and wide prestige and determinedly delegate to him or her the authority to manage the organization. It would be helpful if the person in this position were accorded special rank that would give him or her authority over the various under-secretaries-general and encourage permanent representatives to go to him rather than to the Secretary-General with their administrative requests.

These are all changes or improvements that a Secretary-General, with the cooperation and support of members (and of his own staff) can make without any increase in his legal authority. Others that are desirable to increase his authority would entail either regulatory change or the concurrence of member states.

Of great importance as the UN becomes ever more deeply involved in peace-building will be the enhancement of the Secretary-General's leadership role within the UN system as a whole. This, as pointed out in an earlier chapter, will be dependent on a restructuring of the system itself, which, depending on its nature, might or might not entail amendment of the Charter.

In the purely administrative area he should also have greater freedom to move positions among the various sections of the program budget in order to meet the needs of the rapidly changing security situations with which the UN must deal. This would require only a decision by the General Assembly to modify the relevant financial regulations.

STRENGTHENING THE SECRETARY-GENERAL'S ABILITY TO ENSURE THE SAFETY OF UN PERSONNEL

Given the prevalence of volatile political situations in countries where UN humanitarian or assistance programs are under way, UN personnel and affiliated NGO staff members find themselves in grave, and often sudden, danger. In the absence of any form of protection, the only conscionable action for the Secretary-General to take, given his responsibility for the safety of UN staff members, is to withdraw the UN personnel and thereby interrupt what may be gravely needed help for a civilian population under threat. In such cases, it would be of high humanitarian and morale value if the Secretary-General had the authority and the capability to quickly send a UN guard contingent adequately trained and armed to afford protection to the UN and, to the extent possible, to other international humanitarian personnel present in the area.

There are precedents for such action. Trygve Lie, the first Secretary-General, after his proposal to form a UN constabulary force had been turned down, sent UN guards to provide protection for UN personnel in Palestine at the time of the first Arab/Israeli war. More recently (and more relevantly) Secretary-General Pérez de Cuéllar sent UN guards to Northern Iraq where the United Nations was seeking to bring humanitarian relief to the Kurdish population that was under attack from the Iraqi Government. Some members of the Security Council had urged that a UN peacekeeping force be sent to the area. The Iraqi authorities refused to give their consent. The Secretary-General therefore proposed, instead, to send UN guards to the area. The guards were ostensibly to provide protection for UN relief centers and UN personnel, but it was also intended that their presence give a sense of security to the Kurdish population. The Iraqis agreed that the guards could be deployed, carrying only side arms. Some 600 were eventually deployed (some were stationed at other points in Iraq) to very good effect both in terms of the safety of UN personnel and of the sense of greater security enjoyed by the Kurds.

Secretary-General Pérez de Cuéllar sent the guards on his own authority. The Security Council had passed a resolution demanding that Iraq allow access to all residents in need of humanitarian assistance. This was seen as a legal justification for the Secretary-General's action, although the legal staff of the Secretariat has never given an opinion on whether such justification was necessary.

UN guards have the status of regular Secretariat staff members. As such they are subject to assignment by the Secretary-General to any UN post. The Secretary-General would be in a stronger position to be of assistance in internal crises if there were a contingent of well-trained guards whom he could dispatch on short notice. They would be recruited by the UN and not provided by contributing countries. Training would be done by the UN. When not needed in emergencies, they could supplement the guard contingents at regular posts or be integrated for special police duties in peace-keeping operations. As was the case in Iraq, local authorities are likely to be more amenable to the dispatch of UN Guards than military peace-keeping personnel. The General Assembly would have to approve the establishment of the additional posts for such a unit and the budget to finance them.

Greater authorization to move positions within the Secretariat and the establishment of a standing UN guard contingent, available for use in emergencies by the Secretary-General—these are two relatively modest ways in which the authority of the Secretary-General could be enlarged to give him a greater capability to deal with the increasingly demanding problems faced by the UN. Neither would involve any Charter modification.[13]

Having said this, it must be added that members have traditionally been reluctant to see the power of the Secretary-General increased. The one suggestion that Secretary-General Boutros-Ghali made in *An Agenda for Peace* that would have slightly enhanced his authority by empowering him to refer a matter to the International Court of Justice was simply ignored by member states. It is by no means certain that there would be approval in the General Assembly even for the steps proposed here.

For the most part, the present Secretary-General, and most likely his successors, will have to fulfill the complex responsibilities of the post–Cold War era through skillful utilization of presently existing authority and through the strength of their resolve, the force of their personality and their communication skills. The importance of the ability to communicate cannot be overemphasized when support for United Nations programs will depend so heavily on persuasion.

With these qualities a Secretary-General can counter, or overcome, many of the obstacles that are an inherent part of the job. There is one, in particular, however, that no Secretary-General will be able to resolve on his own—the obstacle that inadequate resources constitutes for the successful management of the organization and its programs. Major additions in permanent staff may not be necessary to cover expanded regular programs. However, additional funding will be needed to allow the Secretary-General flexibility in the recruitment on a nonpermanent basis of skilled personnel for large peace-keeping and peace-making undertakings, duties that cannot be adequately performed by staff already on the rolls. The funds available for peacekeeping have been dangerously insufficient to the point that, when deployment of a peacekeeping force to Bosnia was agreed to in 1992, the Secretary-General was forced to say that there were no funds available for the action and therefore those countries participating would have to cover their own expenses. If funds are inadequate, the Secretary-General cannot manage the deployment of a peace-keeping operation in such a way as to ensure its timely effectiveness. The resource problem extends to the whole area of peace-building, where the Secretary-General is unable to implement the needed programs if sufficient funding is not available. The relationship between the adequate availability of resources and effective management by the Secretary-General is painfully apparent.

NOTES

1. Dick Thornburgh, "Report to the Secretary-General of the United Nations," March 1, 1993, unpublished. Made available by Mr. Thornburgh.

2. Ruth Russell, *A History of the United Nations Charter* (Washington, D.C.: The Brookings Institution, 1958), p. 371.

3. General Assembly Official Records, Forty-First Session, Supplement 49 (a/41/49), 1986.

4. Dick Thornburgh, "Report to the Secretary-General of the United Nations."

5. GA Resolution 13 (I), 13 February 1946.

6. The Economic and Social Commission for West Asia, now located in Amman, earlier had its headquarters in Baghdad and may return there when conditions are appropriate.

7. In their study "The Reorganization of the United Nations Secretariat," written in February 1991 and published by the Ford Foundation in New York, Brian Urquhart and Erskine Childers state that there are more than thirty units in the Secretariat that are supposed to report directly to the Secretary-General.

8. Lecture delivered at Oxford University, 30 May 1961. UN Document SE/1035, 30 May 1961.

9. Lecture delivered by Secretary-General Pérez de Cuéllar at Oxford University on April 13, 1986.

10. Urquhart and Childers, "A World in Need of Leadership" (Uppsala, Sweden: Dag Hammarskjöld Foundation, 1990), p. 83.

11. Trygve Lie, *In the Cause of Peace* (New York: Macmillan, 1954), p. 45.

12. Report of the Secretary-General on the Work of the Organization, DPI/785–41191–September 1983–12M.

13. UN guards were first employed in the field to afford protection to UN personnel by Secretary-General Trygve Lie at the time of the first Arab/Israeli War. He had earlier proposed the establishment of a UN "constabulary" for guard duty in the Middle East but this idea was rejected by member states.

9

The Challenge for Governments and Peoples

In studies of the ability of the United Nations to meet the challenge of maintaining international security in the circumstances of an essentially new era, there is a frequent tendency to look at the organization as a self-contained entity, capable, in itself, of correcting all the inadequacies that have been evident and of acquiring, through its own endeavors, the means and the capability to respond to the problems of the next fifty years. Such an impression might well have been gained from what is recorded in some of the preceding chapters. But this is not so.

The ability of the United Nations to meet adequately the demands placed on it by present and future world conditions will, of course, depend on the quality and performance of its staff and structure. It will depend even more heavily, however, on the policies of governments and on the attitudes and orientation of populations on which government policies in an era of increasing democracy and transparency are ultimately dependent.

The UN Security Council has become the center for collective decision making regarding threats to international security. The debates there can and do influence the positions of Council members. The consensus or coalition-building process that is part of decision making can cause governments to alter positions. Still, on the substantive issues of international security, the decisions taken by the Council are determined by policy decisions made in capitals. In searching for answers on how the new post–Cold War capacity of the United Nations can be maintained and enhanced, it is necessary to look beyond the UN Headquarters building in New York to national capitals and to world public opinion.

In adjusting to the conditions of the post-Cold War world, governments in the formulation of national security policy have had to come to grips with issues that impact directly on the performance of the United Nations. Many have been engaged in a continuing assessment of the performance and potential of the UN and of the limitations on what it or other organizations or individual states can do in given crisis situations.

THE LIMITS OF INVOLVEMENT

A good many governments, in light of the proliferation of political and social crises within countries (mostly poor and small) and the resultant strain on UN resources, have begun to try to define when there should be UN intervention: e.g., only when success is assured; only when, in the case of conflict, there is a clear will on the part of the combatants to reach a settlement; only when neighboring countries or the appropriate regional organization cannot deal with the situation; only when there is a request from the government in power, or all the parties to an internal conflict, for UN assistance.

It would clearly be easier to reach expeditious decisions in the Security Council on action or inaction if there were agreed guidelines stating clear positions, such as those just cited, on the circumstances under which UN peacekeeping or peace-enforcement operations would be warranted. However, each crisis that arises is *sui generis* involving to a different degree the interests and concerns of individual Council Members. Any guidelines that seek to determine in advance the reaction of the Council to a particular crisis when it arises are likely to be untenable. More importantly, restrictive guidelines, established in the abstract, can jeopardize the ability of the UN to counter a serious threat to human security. If, for example, the Council agreed to intervene only when success is assured, the UN could be placed in the position of watching wanton loss of life because the success of UN action (however that might be defined) is less than certain. Given the complexity and bitterness of some intrastate conflicts, the UN is likely to fail in achieving success in every case. Individual failures, however, should not be seen as negating the value of achievements or the validity of UN endeavors to protect human security.

The criterion for deciding on UN intervention that would most closely accord with the principles of the Charter and the objective of enhancing human security is *the intensity of the need*. How serious will the consequences be for the people of a country or for the peace of the region if the UN does *not* intervene? If there were general agreement that the UN would provide whatever assistance it can to alleviate situations that threaten the lives and property of an appreciable portion of a country or a region's population, there would be a principled basis for future decisions that would not be discriminatory toward any country or people.

The immediate (and negative) response that this approach would prompt in many quarters would be that it would result in UN military operations, whether peacekeeping or peace-enforcement, beyond the UN's capacity. Where would the resources come from? It would be—and has been—argued that the overextension that would likely result would mean an overall decrease in the effectiveness of the UN rather than an enhancement.

As stated at the beginning of this book, continuing intrastate crises deriving from societal tensions must be anticipated. However, the number of occasions for UN military intervention under the criterion suggested above need not be overwhelming. It is within the power of the world community—if the UN, regional organizations, NGO's and governments work together—to limit the intensity of such critical situations through preventive measures and peace-building as described in earlier chapters of this book. Furthermore, with a modification in the understanding of the requirements of national defense, which is discussed in subsequent paragraphs, the troops and resources would be available should there be a further expansion of the need for peacekeeping.

The United Nations Development Program's 1994 Report on Human Development concludes that "early warning signals" of the kind of violence that swept Somalia can be detected now regarding Afghanistan, Angola, Haiti, Iraq, Mozambique, Burma, Sudan and Zaire. If these early warning signals are heeded a repetition of the Somalia experience need not occur. There must, however, be a fundamental change in the way developing countries budget their government resources and in the way more advanced industrialized countries allocate foreign aid.[1]

RESOURCES

To seek to prevent intrastate crises or at least to lessen their intensity will not, unfortunately, eliminate the problem of resources. Prophylaxis can be even more costly than emergency treatment, although the cost can be offset by the ultimate returns. But there are potential sources of additional funds. The real reduction in military expenditures that is occurring in both developed and developing countries can make substantial resources available to be applied toward essential human security goals if governments so decide. According to UN statistics, defense spending in developed countries fell from 850 billion dollars in 1987 to an estimated 649 billion dollars in 1994, a drop of some 23 percent. During the same period military expenditures in the poorer developing countries declined by 19 percent, from 145 billion dollars to 118 billion. Utilization of a portion of these savings to meet human security goals through such means as primary health care and the elimination of severe malnutrition, basic family planning and the reduction of illiteracy could materially lessen the likelihood of intense intrastate social crises over the next fifty years.

Savings from the reduction in military expenditures is not the only possible source of additional funds for human development. The Nobel Prize-winning economist, Professor James Tobin, has suggested (as have others) the imposition of a fee on speculative transactions in currency markets as a means of gaining the needed resources. UNDP has proposed a "20:20 compact" in which developing countries undertake to devote 20 percent of their budgets and industrial countries designate 20 percent of their aid to "human priority expenditures" as a means of achieving sustained human security development.[2]

Not all intrastate conflicts are the result of inadequate social and economic development. Some stem from ethnic tensions and human rights violations that will not necessarily be eliminated by preventive measures of an essentially economic nature. While other kinds of preventive measures can be applied when early warning signs are detected, it would be illusory to think that all conflicts can be prevented and the need for UN intervention completely eliminated. Through far-sighted government policies, however, it is possible to reduce the likely number. It is not inevitable that the UN will be overwhelmed by an escalating number of crises.

THE MISSION OF NATIONAL MILITARY FORCES

The greatly expanded need for peace-keeping and peace-enforcement operations raises questions about how the mission of national military forces should be defined in the post–Cold War era. Such operations are becoming so extensive as to outstrip the willingness and/or the capability of traditional contributing countries to provide the needed personnel. The costs are so high as to meet the increasing resistance of governments making payments they do not see as directly related to their national security. Moreover, the increased sensitivity and danger inherent in enforcement actions is causing reluctance on the part of some governments to see their troops or civilians involved.

This reluctance reflects public attitudes that, while generally in favor of peacekeeping, can quickly become negative in the face of media coverage of peace-keeping soldiers being killed—or killing local nationals—in behalf of the vaguely understood concept of international security. When the Security Council resolved that an additional 7,500 troops should be sent to Bosnia to protect the safe areas designated by the Council, the Secretary-General found member states reluctant to volunteer forces and a considerable delay resulted in their deployment, notwithstanding the evident urgency of the need. This problem is sufficiently serious to jeopardize the ability of the United Nations to take forceful measures for peace. The expanded resort to the UN for military action to preserve peace calls for nothing less than a modification of the traditional understanding of the mission of national defense.

Some change is already apparent. U.S. Presidential Decision Directive 25 amounts to official U.S. acceptance of the principle that UN peace-keeping and enforcement measures may be taken for the maintenance of human security as well as interstate security. The military enforcement action led by the United States, at considerable cost in defense resources, to provide security for humanitarian assistance in Somalia did not serve U.S. national defense, or the national defense of the twenty other countries that participated. Rather, the military undertaking was in the cause of human security. France, with the less than unanimous approval of the Security Council, took comparable, though more modest, action to limit the humanitarian tragedy in Rwanda (although it can be argued that certain narrow French national interests were involved in the French decision). There was widespread public support in the United States and France for the action taken by the two governments for humanitarian reasons. The effect on the national conscience of mass suffering, clear for all to see on television, has been shown to be considerable.

The American and French actions were, however, taken under national leadership and at the initiative of the national government. When leadership of the Somali action was transferred to the United Nations and American soldiers were killed, the United States withdrew and subsequently declared that it would provide troops for peace-keeping and peace-enforcement missions only when it served the U.S. national interest.

It can be taken as a given that the first goal of national defense establishments will remain defense of the homeland and its citizens. With the disappearance of the Cold War as the determining factor in the national defense policies of the major military powers, protection from the adverse impact of regional conflicts, whether interstate or intrastate, has become a principal purpose of national defense. If the main action to counter regional conflicts in the future is to be multilateral, under the leadership or auspices of the United Nations, then an important aspect of national defense is the strengthening, militarily, of the United Nations. Following this reasoning, greater resources from national defense establishments should be allocated to the United Nations for peace-keeping and peace-enforcement operations. This must entail some restructuring of national defense forces in order to accommodate the requirements of further enlarged UN peace-keeping and peace-enforcement operations. The acceptance of serious risks of casualties, until now justifiable in most countries only for defense of the homeland, must become justifiable for peace in intrastate and interstate conflicts and for the safety of populations threatened by genocide or other massive violations of basic human rights.

THE NATIONAL INTEREST

Underlying all such issues as the allocation of resources, support for a stronger UN and participation in UN peace-enforcement operations is the question of national interest. How is "the national interest" to be defined in an era of increasing interdependence and altered security threats?

It is universally accepted that the first concern of a nation's leaders must be protection of its national interests. This is frequently posed in a way to suggest that there is a contradiction between the national interest and the wider interests of the global community. This suggestion comes through most starkly in debates heard frequently in major countries as to why they should be concerned with conflicts, or the massive infringement of human rights, in small, far-off countries. American soldiers, President Clinton decided, will participate in UN peace-keeping and peace-enforcement actions only when this serves the "national interest." Some Third World countries reject environmental reforms as contrary to the national interest. It is understandable, and inevitable, that a Canadian family that has lost a son or daughter trying to bring peace between people in a distant country fighting largely because of mutual hatred will ask "How does this serve *our* national interest?" Is there justification for the expenditure of millions and even billions of dollars to bring humanitarian assistance to people who seemingly cannot govern themselves?

It is not to be expected that the national interest will cease to be the principal determining factor in the formulation of national policy. No free government will willingly pursue a policy that is contrary to national interest as its people understand it, or remain long in office if it does. That is why it is of such importance that "national interest" be understood and defined in terms that are compatible with efforts to build a world at peace in the post–Cold War environment. It is relatively easy to see that there is a national interest in countries with high and low birthrates in controlling fertility. On such macro issues as the environment and disease control there is unquestionably a growing fusion of national and global interests. For this reason the United Nations has had, and will continue to have, success in mobilizing support for global programs in these fields.

The threat for UN security programs lies more in national attitudes toward seemingly country- or region-specific issues. The answer to the age-old question "am I my brother's keeper?" has to be yes, because it is in national interest that my brother (and sister) be safe and well and at peace. This is first of all a question of ethics. It is in the national interest of every country that the coming century be a century in which ethical considerations figure in the shaping of government policies and of global public opinion. All countries and peoples will be safer as a result.

It is in the interest of the United States and Russia and Brazil and every other country that genocide be stopped wherever it occurs, because if nothing is done not only will many thousands of fellow humans die, but cynicism will gain in force. Cynicism works against success in building peace. It is thus contrary to the national interest of every country and people.

There are more pragmatic reasons why it is in the national interest of developed countries to participate with resources and, when necessary, troops and equipment, in resolving human security crises in poorer countries. No matter how distant they may be, migrants fleeing conflict and social chaos will eventually reach the shores of the rich in numbers too large to be easily absorbed. Terrorist movements born in resistance to intolerable conditions in one country will spread their bases and exert a disruptive influence on social tranquility in third countries. These are only two of the many diseases of interdependence that it is in the national interest of every country to cure.

The goal of bringing about fundamental changes in public thinking and government policies on the mission of national defense establishments and on the allocation of resources in the interest of human security is audacious, to say the least. To many the equation of ethics with national interest will be confounding (although it is an underlying assumption of the UN Charter). But the international constellation at present is unique in history both in the opportunities it offers to enhance international security, and in the terrible evidence it displays of the dangers of not exploiting them.

It was no doubt presumptuous of George Bush and Mikhail Gorbachev to speak glowingly of a new world order without defining very clearly what it would be or providing useful guidance on how to get there. They were right, though, in sensing that great changes were in the making. It would be an enduring tragedy if this new era were characterized by retrogression into chaos because of a failure to perceive that the well-being of societies is interlinked and demands common efforts in behalf of human security. This is the time to ensure that resources are made available in sufficient measure to afford the United Nations the credibility it must have if it is to be a major and effective force for peace.

NOTES

1. United Nations Development Program, The Human Development Report (New York and Oxford: Oxford University Press, 1994), pp. 41–32.
2. Ibid., pp. 7–8.

Selected Bibliography

Baehr, Peter R., and Leon Gordenker. *The United Nations in the 1990's*. New York: St. Martin's Press, 1992.

Blechman, Barry M., and J. Matthew Vaccoro. *Training for Peacekeeping, The United Nations' Role*. Washington, D.C.: Henry L. Stimson Center, 1994.

Boulden, Jane. *Prometheus Unborn: The History of the Military Staff Committee*. Ottawa: Canadian Centre For Global Security, 1993.

Boutros-Ghali, Boutros. *Report of the Secretary-General on the Work of the Organization to the Forty-seventh Session of the General Assembly*. United Nations, 1992.

Boutros-Ghali, Boutros. *An Agenda for Peace*. United Nations, 1993.

Claude, Inis, Jr. *Swords into Plowshares*. New York: Random House, 1984.

Cox, David. *Exploring An Agenda for Peace*. Ottawa: Canadian Center for Global Security, 1993.

Diehl, Paul F. *International Peacekeeping*. Baltimore: Johns Hopkins University Press, 1993.

Durch, William J. *The Evolution of UN Peacekeeping*. New York: St. Martin's Press, 1993.

Goodrich, Leland. *The Charter of the United Nations*. Boston: World Peace Foundation, 1949.

Gordenker, Leon, and Benjamin Rivlin, eds. *The Challenging Role of the UN Secretary-General*. Westport, CT: Praeger, 1993.

Kennedy, Paul. *Preparing for the Twenty-first Century*. New York: Random House, 1993.

Lie, Trygve. *In the Cause of Peace*. New York: Macmillan, 1954.

Pérez de Cuéllar, Javier. *Anarchy or Order*. United Nations, 1991.

Russell, Ruth. *A History of the United Nations Charter*. Washington, D.C.: The Brookings Institution, 1958.

Russett, Bruce. *Grasping the Democratic Peace*. Princeton, NJ: Princeton University Press, 1993.

Stettinius, Edward R., Jr. *Report to the President on the San Francisco Conference*. Washington, D.C.: Department of State, 1945.

United Nations. *The Blue Helmets*. New York: United Nations, 1990.

Urquhart, Brian. *Dag Hammarskjöld*. New York: Knopf, 1972.

Wiess, Thomas G., ed. *Collective Security in a Changing World*. Boulder and London: Lynne Reinner, 1993.

Williams, Douglas. *The Specialized Agencies and the United Nations*. London: Hurst, 1987.

The World Commission on Environment and Development. *Our Common Future*. New York: The Oxford Press, 1987.

Index

96–98; potential of, 93–111; and
   UN advantage, 102–8
Resources: and availability of Secre-
   tary-General, 122; of UN, 135–36
Russia, 98

Safety of UN personnel, 129–31
San Francisco Conference in 1945, 19
Secretary-General, 113–32; assessing
   performance of, 115–16; coordinat-
   ing system of, 124–25; and free-
   dom of action, 119–24;
   improvements for, 125–29; and
   post–Cold War relations, 116; and
   safety of UN personnel, 129–31;
   staff of, 117–19; and UN admini-
   stration, 117
Security Council, 3, 4–6, 8–9
Social development, 4; as peace-build-
   ing, 78
Somalia, 8, 59–63, 63–65, 66, 73
South Asia, 108
Southern Lebanon, 32–36
South Georgia Island, 14
Soviet Union, 6, 14, 115
Staff of Secretary-General, 117–19,
   122–24
Stettinius, Edward, 4, 93
Structure and organizations, multilat-
   eral nuclear alert center, 90–91
Swords into Plowshares, 74

Thant, U, 29, 115
Thornburgh, Dick, 113, 117
Tobin, James, 136
Training and peace enforcement, 66
Truman, Harry, 94

Ukraine, 88
UN Specialized Agencies, 124

UNFICYP (United Nations Force in
   Cyprus), 29–32
UNIFIL (United Nations Interim
   Force in Lebanon), 32–36
UNTAG (United Nations Transitional
   Assistance Group), 36–38
United Kingdom, 13–14
United Nations: administration of,
   117; advantage over regional organizations, 102–8; and difference
   from League of Nations, 4; limits
   of involvement, 134–35; maintain-
   ing international security, 133–39;
   and national interest, 138–39; new
   challenges of, 7–8; and new rules
   of game, 8–9; and past weak-
   nesses, 4–6; resources of, 135–36;
   and time of progress, 6
United Nations Development Program's 1994 Report on Human Development, 135
United Nations Emergency Force
   (UNEF), 26
United States, 14, 87; participation in
   League of Nations, 3–4
USSR, 87

Vance, Cyrus, 18, 23

Waldheim, Kurt, 33, 108
Welles, Sumner, 2
Western European Union (WEU), 99–
   102, 106
Woerner, Manfred, 101
World Bank, 80

Yugoslavia, 7–8, 22–23, 95, 102–3; and
   European regional organizations,
   98–102; and peace-enforcement,
   56–58

About the Author

JAMES S. SUTTERLIN is a fellow at Yale University and Adjunct Professor of Political Science at Long Island University. After serving as Inspector General of the U.S. Foreign Service, Professor Sutterlin joined the UN Secretariat, where during the tenure of Secretary-General Pérez de Cuéllar, he was Director of the Secretary General's office. He has written widely on UN affairs and is currently Chairman of the Board of Directors of the Academic Council on the United Nations.

ISBN 0-275-95052-2

90000>

EAN

9 780275 950521

HARDCOVER BAR CODE